MW01041625

Open Court Reading
SRA
Genre Practice

Grade 5

McGraw Hill Education

mheducation.com/prek-12

Copyright © 2018 McGraw-Hill Education

Send all inquiries to:
McGraw-Hill Education
8787 Orion Place
Columbus, OH 43240

ISBN: 978-0-07-682502-8
MHID: 0-07-682502-7

Printed in the United States of America

3 4 5 6 7 8 9 LHS 26 25 24 23 22

Table of Contents

Emily's Secret

Read the passage below. Then answer the questions that follow.

Soledad was planning to spend the night at her friend Emily's house on Friday, and they were both looking forward to the sleepover. They were talking about their plans in the school lunchroom Wednesday when Emily began giggling.

"Oh, Soledad," Emily laughed, "I'll have a surprise waiting when you come over on Friday, but I don't want to give it away."

"Come on, Emily," Soledad smiled, "I'm no detective! Tell me!"

"See if you can guess," Emily teased, as the bell rang calling them back to class.

All afternoon, Soledad wondered about Emily's secret. How was she supposed to unravel the mystery, especially if Emily refused to give her any clues? But she was determined to get to the bottom of it before the sleepover on Friday night.

Thursday at lunch, the girls sat together as usual. As she unpacked her lunchbox, Soledad noticed some scratches on Emily's arm and hand, and she asked what caused them.

"It's no big deal," Emily replied, gulping down some milk. "I just got scratched up a bit when I was–" She stopped abruptly. "Oops, I don't want to tell any more. You'll find out tomorrow night. Hey, what kind of fruit did you bring today?"

Whenever Soledad asked about the marks on Emily's arm, Emily changed the subject. Soledad knew it had something to do with Emily's secret—though it didn't sound like a very nice surprise if it might leave scratches on her arm! She was about to ask once more when Emily interrupted her:

"Aren't you going to finish your sandwich? That looks like tuna fish, right? Can I have the rest . . . I mean, if you're not going to eat it, that is."

Soledad grinned as she handed over the last bit of her sandwich. "You must be extra hungry today, huh?" she chuckled. But to her surprise, Emily tossed it in her lunchbox and closed the lid.

"This'll come in handy later," Emily cried, jumping up from the table. "Come on, it's almost time to get back to the classroom." She ran out of the lunchroom, Soledad trailing behind her. "Hey wait! Why did you want my . . . come in handy for what? Emily!"

Because they were busy with testing all afternoon, Soledad didn't get a chance to talk to Emily the rest of the day, and when Soledad looked for Emily to walk home after school, she was nowhere to be found. As Soledad walked home by herself, her phone buzzed—it was a text from Emily.

"Sorry I had to run," Emily's text began, "but I had to get home to take care of something. I'll stop by your house tomorrow before school."

Soledad was more puzzled than ever. Why was Emily acting so strangely . . . and why did she need to get home so quickly? She texted Emily back, but Emily just answered, "Busy, see you tomorrow!" Was this all part of Emily's secret?

Soledad was still confused the next morning when Emily knocked on her door.

"Good morning!" Emily said brightly. "Tonight's our sleepover and you'll finally get to see my surprise!"

Soledad was about to answer when she noticed a patch of orange fur clinging to Emily's shirt. Suddenly, it all made sense. She reached out and picked the fur from Emily's shirt.

"Does this have something to do with the surprise?" Soledad laughed, waving the fur in Emily's face. "And the little scratches, too?"

Emily started to giggle.

"So . . . did your new kitty enjoy my tuna-fish sandwich?"

Emily nodded, smiling broadly. "Her name's Maya! I can't wait for you to meet her!" The girls chattered excitedly the rest of the way to school.

Writing to Sources • *Genre Practice*

Name _____ Date _____

Respond to Reading

**Read each question, then write your answers on the lines.
For questions that ask you to underline text evidence, mark
your answers on pages 1–2.**

1. Underline text evidence in the story that shows Emily is being secretive.

2. Reread the excerpt in the box:

> All afternoon, Soledad wondered about Emily's secret. How was she supposed to *unravel* the mystery, especially if Emily refused to give her any clues? But she was determined to get to the bottom of it before the sleepover on Friday night.

Use context clues to write a synonym for *unravel*. Which phrase in the paragraph has the same meaning as *unravel*?

_____

_____

_____

3. What does Emily mean when she says Soledad's tuna fish sandwich will "come in handy later"? How do you know?

_____

_____

_____

4. How would you react if a close friend teased you by keeping a secret from you?

_____

_____

_____

5. Explain how Soledad finally puts together all the pieces of evidence that allow her to uncover Emily's secret.

_____

_____

_____

6. Write a brief text message in the box below You will be Soledad responding to Emily's text. List events from the story, outside of the box, that tell you how Soledad feels after she reads Emily's text.

```
┌─────────────────────────────────────────┐
│  ================================         │
│                                           │
│  Emily                                    │
│                                           │
│  Sorry I had to run, but I had to get home to take │
│  care of something. I'll stop by your house │
│  tomorrow before school.                  │
│                                           │
│  ================================         │
│                                           │
│                              Soledad      │
│                                           │
│                                           │
│                                           │
│                                           │
│                                           │
│                                           │
│                                           │
│                                           │
└─────────────────────────────────────────┘
```

Writing to Sources • *Genre Practice*

The Birds of Fenice

Read the passage below. Then answer the questions that follow.

I shouldn't have climbed to the top of the bell tower in the first place. My parents have told me time and time again that 11-year-old girls should not climb, which only makes me want to do it more. Besides, lying out on sunbaked roof tiles is better than lurking in the dark alleys where the other children play. Dark places scare me, but rooftops don't.

The village of Fenice was built at the end of a rugged peninsula. Most of the buildings were three or four stories tall, made of brick and timber, and crammed together. The one building that stood apart from the rest was the bell tower, which loomed in the town's center.

A month ago, I made the difficult climb to its top, and was stunned by the spectacular views. I was also reminded that the bell tower was sealed tight. The doors at the bottom were locked, and the openings at the top were shuttered. No one in Fenice remembered why.

If I had left the shutters closed, everything would have been different. But my curiosity was like an itch that only got worse and worse, until I had to know what was inside so badly it almost hurt. I ripped the shutters open and unleashed a torrent of birds that nearly knocked me from the wall. Their bright, metallic orange feathers glimmered in the sunlight. As the flock wheeled around and soared closer, I could hear they were talking!

Suddenly, a nearby voice chirped, "Hello," startling me so much, I nearly fell a second time. When I recovered, one bird who had remained in the roost introduced himself as Henry. He explained, rather embarrassedly, that he was afraid of heights, and asked if I could help him down. So I tucked Henry in my pocket and descended the tower.

Initially, the village rejoiced. The birds were welcomed with a banquet, rich with food and entertainment. The people and the birds of Fenice celebrated new bonds of friendship that they promised would last forever.

This changed quickly when it became clear the birds had ravenous appetites. They began taking food from outdoor tables, and then indoor tables, and then pantries and cabinets. And they were so ungrateful! The birds would steal your fish sandwich and then grumble that it wasn't a cheese sandwich, and then, they would eat your cheese and moan about that, too.

All of the birds complained, except for Henry, who had become my best friend.

People did their best to cope. Store owners batted the birds with brooms. Residents shooed them away with their hands. However, when the birds became agitated, they exploded into a ball of flame. Several buildings burned down. With no more food, and no way to make the birds leave, people began to abandon the village.

"How can I fix this mess I created?" I asked Henry.

That's when Henry told me about the bell in the tower, which when rung, would call the birds back to the tower where they could again be sealed inside. The next day, we climbed the tower. At the top, I gazed into the tower's dark depths and froze with fright. "I'm afraid of the dark."

Henry said he would light the way. Before I could object, he worked himself into a frenzy about his fellow birds' rude behavior, making himself so agitated that he burst into flames.

Henry's glowing embers provided enough light for me to find the bell and ring it. The birds returned to their roosts, and the village was saved.

Fantasy • *Genre Practice*

Respond to Reading

Read each question. Circle the letter next to your answer choice.

1. Which genre best describes this passage?

   a. biography

   b. fantasy

   c. historical fiction

   d. science fiction

2. Read the following excerpt.

   > Initially, the village rejoiced. The birds were welcomed with a *banquet*, rich with food and entertainment. The people and the birds of Fenice celebrated new bonds of friendship that they promised would last forever.

   Based on the text, what does the word *banquet* mean?

   f. beverage

   g. cheer

   h. feast

   j. trophy

3. Which sentence best shows the village's problems?

   a. The doors at the bottom were locked, and the openings at the top shuttered.

   b. All of the birds complained, except for Henry, who had become my best friend.

   c. With no more food, and no way to make the birds leave, people began to abandon the village.

   d. The birds returned to their roosts, and the village was saved.

4. Which of these is the best summary of the passage?

   f. A girl accidentally unleashes destructive talking birds onto her village. She befriends one of the birds, Henry. Together they return the birds to their roost.

   g. A girl climbs to the top of a bell tower and discovers a group of talking birds. Their leader, Henry, invites the narrator to a large banquet in her honor.

   h. Talking birds escape from their roost in the bell tower. They eat the village's food, burn down its buildings, and force the people to abandon their homes.

   j. A talking bird named Henry befriends a girl. Together they overcome his fear of the dark and her fear of heights by climbing the village's bell tower.

Reread the last six paragraphs on page 6. Pay attention to the order of events.

Think about how the plot develops in this selection. Organize your ideas. Use the space below for prewriting.

Write a response on a separate piece of paper. What happens in these last six paragraphs? Why would the author write the events in this order? Give evidence from the selection to support your ideas.

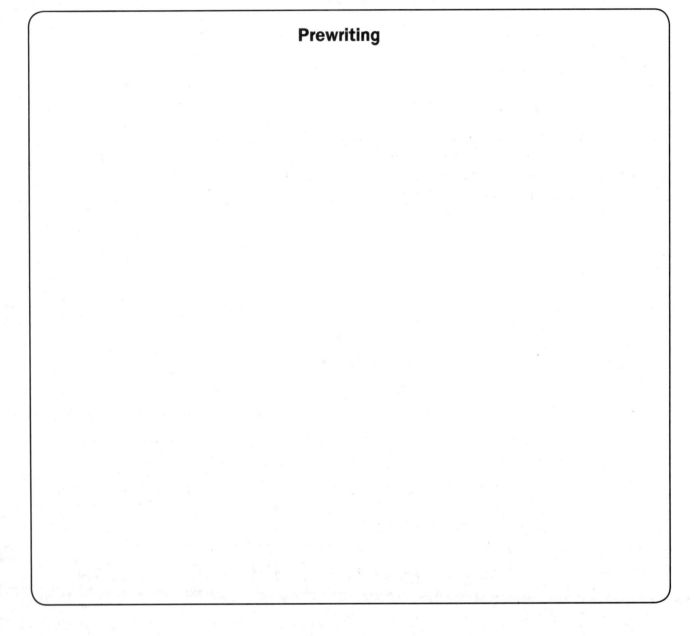

Prewriting

Be sure to—

1. include details that describe the events and their sequence.

2. organize your writing.

3. use your own words.

4. use correct spelling, capitalization, punctuation, grammar, and complete sentences.

Fantasy • *Genre Practice*

Paper or Plastic?

Read the passage below. Then answer the questions that follow.

As you begin to unload your cart of groceries, the cashier turns to you and asks, "Paper or plastic?" You wonder whether one is better for the environment than the other. Should you request paper bags or plastic ones? The answer is neither. The best choice for the environment is to supply your own reusable bags.

Reusable bags are exactly what their name suggests—reusable. You buy them once and then use them again and again. Using reusable bags when you shop helps the environment by reducing the amount of waste in landfills and pollution in the air and waterways.

Both paper bags and plastic bags cause air and water pollution. Even though paper bags are made from trees, the process to turn wood into paper requires the use of toxic chemicals. The same is true for the production of plastic bags. They are made mostly from oil. Surprisingly, though, the manufacturing of paper bags causes 70% more air pollution and 50% more water pollution than the manufacturing of plastic bags. While paper bags may create more air and water pollution, plastic bags pose a greater threat to ocean animals. Because plastic bags are lightweight and can easily blow around in the wind, they often end up in the ocean. There, animals, such as turtles, mistake the bags for food and end up dying due to choking or blocked intestines.

Paper bags and plastic bags are also filling our landfills. Because paper bags are made from trees, they are biodegradable. They can break down, but only if they have the right conditions. Water, light, oxygen, and other elements are needed. Since most of the waste in landfills is buried under dirt, the paper bags are unable to break down completely. Plastic bags are not made from natural products. They are not biodegradable. When plastic bags are thrown in the trash, they stay in the trash.

Reusable bags are not without their faults. Like paper bags and plastic bags, reusable bags make an impact on the environment. Some are made from plastic or with the use of toxic chemicals. Some are produced in other countries and then transported hundreds of miles, which takes a lot of energy. However, when people make it a habit to use their reusable bags, they then reduce the bags' environmental impact. In fact, the steady use of one cloth bag can take the place of 1,000 plastic bags.

The phrase "steady use" is key. In order for reusable bags to help the environment, people like you must make it a habit to use them when shopping for groceries, clothes, or anything else. Keeping reusable bags handy in the car or at home helps. That way, you'll have them for your next visit to the grocery store. And when the cashier asks if you'd like paper or plastic, you can respond, "No thanks, I brought my own reusable bags."

Argumentative Text • *Genre Practice*

Respond to Reading

Read each question. Circle the letter next to your answer choice.

1. This passage is an argumentative text because it—

    a. discusses three different bags.

    b. tells the pros and cons of each bag.

    c. explains how each bag is produced.

    d. gives facts and opinions about each type of bag.

2. How does the comparison of the different bags in the fifth paragraph support the author's argument?

    f. It suggests that paper, plastic, and reusable bags should be made without chemicals.

    g. It reveals the advantage reusable bags have over paper and plastic bags.

    h. It explains how paper, plastic, and reusable bags harm the environment.

    j. It states the reason reusable bags are sometimes produced in other countries.

3. Read the following excerpt.

    > Because paper bags are made from trees, they are *biodegradable.* They can break down, but only if they have the right conditions. Water, light, oxygen, and other elements are needed.

    What does the word *biodegradable* mean?

    a. capable of rot

    c. able to come together

    b. requiring oxygen

    d. losing shape

4. Which sentence best expresses the author's main argument?

    f. The production of paper, plastic, and reusable bags creates pollution.

    g. Paper bags that end up in landfills add to the waste.

    h. Reusable bags are better for the environment than paper or plastic bags.

    j. Ocean animals can be harmed by plastic bags.

Reread the last paragraph of "Paper or Plastic?" on page 10.

Think about the audience for the closing paragraph and what the author wants from the audience. Organize your ideas. Use the space below for prewriting.

Write a response in which you answer this question: *Why is the last paragraph important to the author's argument?* Provide evidence from the passage to support your ideas. Use your own piece of paper.

Prewriting

Be sure to—

1. explain why the final paragraph is important to the argument.

2. include evidence from the passage.

3. connect ideas using linking words, such as *also, another,* and *but.*

4. use correct spelling, capitalization, punctuation, and grammar.

Argumentative Text • *Genre Practice*

The Talking Cat of Tante Odette

Read the passage below. Then answer the questions that follow.

Long ago and far away, an old woman named Tante Odette lived with her gray cat, Chouchou. One evening, as the two were sitting by the fire, a loud knock was heard at the door. When Tante answered the door, she found a strange old man who wore a red sash around his waist and a black feather in his cap.

The man introduced himself as Pierre Leblanc. He told Tante that he was looking for work, but Tante wasn't interested. She began to close the door but stopped when Pierre pointed to Chouchou and said, "Why don't you ask him if you should hire me?"

"Don't be ridiculous!" said Tante. "Cats can't talk."

But to Tante's surprise, Chouchou spoke. "Oh, but I can when there is something important to say. This man looks to be a good, hard worker. You should hire him."

Tante stared at Chouchou for two minutes before she said, "Well, come in, Pierre. It's not every day that a cat talks, so I must listen to him."

Once Pierre was inside, Chouchou spoke twice more, directing Tante to offer Pierre some soup and a place to sleep. Tante was hesitant at first but finally obliged, giving Pierre a bowl of cabbage soup and directing him to the loft in which to rest.

Once Pierre was settled, Tante placed Chouchou in her lap. "After all these years, why start talking now, Chouchou?" But Chouchou said nothing. He merely closed his eyes and began to purr.

Weeks passed, and Pierre proved to be a good worker. One evening, as he ate the soup he received in exchange for work, Chouchou spoke again. "A working man needs more than cabbage soup. He needs meat pies."

Tante argued that meat cost money, but Chouchou replied, "What is money for but to spend? Money cannot keep you warm. You cannot burn it for heat. Give some coins to Pierre, and he will buy us what we need." Tante followed Chouchou's advice. From then on, Pierre made sure they had good food.

One day, while Pierre was chopping wood in the forest, a stranger knocked on Tante's door. He asked if she knew a man by the name of Pierre Leblanc who wore a red sash and had a black feather. Tante said she did. The stranger then asked if her Pierre—for there are many who have the name and wear red sashes and have black feathers—was able to throw his voice. Tante was confused, so the man explained that the Pierre he knew could throw his voice behind trees and make it seem like someone else was speaking. Tante was horrified. She told the man she would never have someone in her house who could do such a tricky thing.

Just then, Pierre appeared, and when the stranger saw him, he broke out in a smile. "Ah, Pierre! There you are. I want you to come trapping with me."

Tante turned to Chouchou. "Chouchou, what does this mean? Our Pierre must be the tricky Pierre who can throw his voice."

Chouchou replied, "Don't be silly. Pierre is helpful and kind. He does not throw his voice. No one can do that."

Tante was relieved, for she enjoyed Pierre's company. She asked Pierre if he was going to leave with the stranger. Pierre responded that he would stay if she would pay him a few coins for his work. Tante agreed, and Pierre walked the stranger outside.

Tante looked down at Chouchou. "I believe we made a good bargain. Don't you?" But Chouchou said nothing. He merely closed his eyes and purred.

Respond to Reading

Read each question. Circle the letter next to your answer choice.

1. This passage is a folktale because it—
   - **a.** involves people interacting with an animal in an unusual way.
   - **b.** has a hero and a villain.
   - **c.** exaggerates a real event.
   - **d.** explains something in nature.

2. Read the following excerpt.

   > Chouchou spoke twice more, directing Tante to offer Pierre some soup and a place to sleep. Tante was hesitant at first but finally *obliged,* giving Pierre a bowl of cabbage soup and directing him to the loft in which to rest.

   Based on the text, what does the word *obliged* mean?
   - **f.** suggested an action
   - **g.** did something as a favor
   - **h.** took something as a warning
   - **j.** refused responsibility

3. The reader can conclude that Pierre—
   - **a.** steals Tante's money.
   - **b.** wants the stranger to stay.
   - **c.** is a lazy worker.
   - **d.** is the voice of Chouchou.

4. Which sentence from the passage best represents the message of the folktale?
   - **f.** "Oh, but I can when there is something important to say."
   - **g.** "What is money for but to spend?"
   - **h.** "Our Pierre must be the tricky Pierre who can throw his voice."
   - **j.** "I believe we made a good bargain."

Reread the seventh paragraph on page 13 and the last paragraph on page 14.

Think about what the sentences tell the reader. Organize your ideas. Use the graphic organizer below for prewriting.

Write a response in which you explain why the author repeats these sentences: "But Chouchou said nothing. He merely closed his eyes and purred." Give evidence from the passage to support your explanation. Use your own piece of paper.

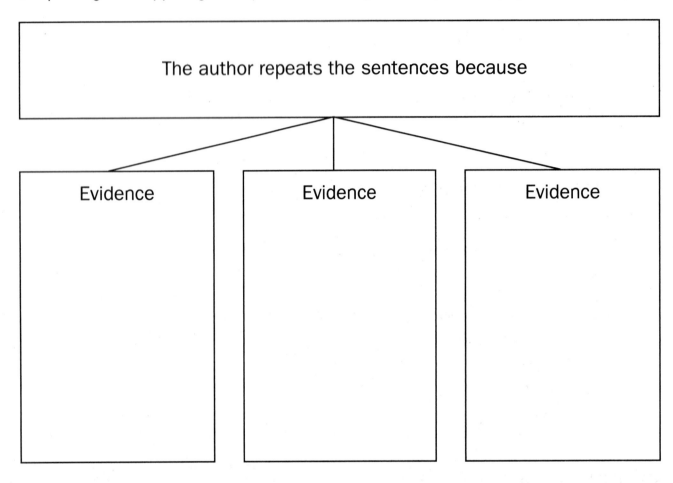

The author repeats the sentences because

Evidence

Evidence

Evidence

Be sure to—

1. explain why the author repeats sentences.

2. provide evidence from the passage.

3. use linking words, such as *also*, *another*, and *but*.

4. use correct spelling, capitalization, punctuation, and grammar.

English: The World's Language

**Read the passage below. Then answer the questions
that follow.**

English has truly become the world's language, spoken by as many as one-quarter of all the people on Earth. It is the common language in business and politics, not to mention entertainment and the Internet, where 80 percent of the stored information is in English. According to Mark Warschauer, a professor at the University of California, "It's gotten to the point where almost in any part of the world, to be educated means to know English."

But how did English become so dominant? Why has English become the "international language"? After all, there are more native speakers of Mandarin Chinese, for example, than English. What makes English so special?

The answer begins in the 17th century, when English was the language of the world's predominant colonial nation—Great Britain. Wherever the British extended their rule, English quickly became the language of commerce and law. By the late 19th century, the British Empire ruled over nearly one-quarter of the world: Canada and the Caribbean; much of South Asia, including India, Hong Kong, and Singapore; Egypt, South Africa, and other parts of Africa; and Australia and New Zealand. And of course, English was the primary language in the United States—itself a former part of the British Empire.

In the mid-18th century, another development had an enormous impact on the spread of English: the birth of the Industrial Revolution in Great Britain. Technological advances such as large-scale manufacturing and production machinery were developed there. New scientific and technological terms were invented. People in other countries who wanted this information needed to learn English to access it, making the language important and essential. It is estimated that between 1750 and 1900 as much as two-thirds of all important scientific and technological advances were written in English.

British imperial and industrial power had introduced English to all corners of the world between the 17th and 19th centuries. By the beginning of the 20th century, however, another player was helping to spread the language even more dramatically: the United States, which had emerged as an economic and political power to rival Great Britain. Under American leadership, the world's nations began to form international organizations—such as the League of Nations (1920) and the United Nations (1945)—and members needed to be able to talk with one another. Most groups chose English as the primary medium of communication.

Since the end of World War II, the economic and cultural dominance of the United States has cemented the international status of English as the world's language. Business deals with U.S. companies are in English. American music, movies, and television are consumed everywhere in the world. In particular, the development of computer and information technology and the rise of the Internet have made it essential for people around the globe to use and understand English. As an article in The New York Times stated, "If you want to take full advantage of the Internet there is only one way to do it: learn English, which has more than ever become America's greatest and most effective export."

As the world becomes more globalized, it will become even more important for people everywhere to be able to communicate with one another. No other language is in a better position to satisfy this need than English, the world's language.

Timeline of Milestones up to Present Day

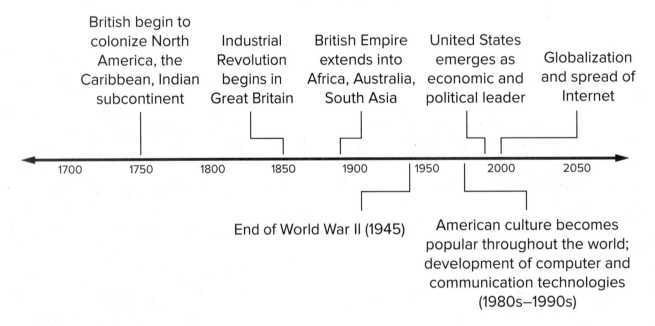

Informational Text • *Genre Practice*

Respond to Reading

Read each question. Circle the letter next to your answer choice.

1. This article is an example of informational text because it—
   a. contains facts that can be verified in another source.
   b. is meant to persuade readers to act in a certain way.
   c. uses imagination to draw the reader into the story.
   d. mainly discusses events that happened in the past.

2. Based on the timeline, which is a correct inference?
   f. The growth of English worldwide has slowed since the early 2000s.
   g. British influence in the United States weakened during the Industrial Revolution.
   h. English was not a world language until the development of the Internet.
   j. The British Empire declined in the years following World War II.

3. Read the following sentence.

   > Since the end of World War II, the economic and cultural dominance of the United States has cemented the international status of English as the world's language.

   Based on the text, which word could you correctly substitute for the word *cemented*?
   a. undermined   c. strengthened
   b. finalized   d. authorized

4. What is the best summary of this article?
   f. Economic, political, and cultural power have made English an international language.
   g. More people in the world speak English than any other language on Earth.
   h. A language becomes widely used if it has a large, descriptive vocabulary.
   j. English is "the world's language" because it is fun and easy to learn.

Reread the article "English: The World's Language" on pages 17–18.

Think about the author's purpose for writing this article. How did the author present the information? How did this contribute to the author's purpose? Organize your ideas. Use the space below for prewriting.

Write about the reasons the author believes English has become the world's language. Which reasons does the author seem to think are most important? How does the way the article is written and the words that are used give you clues about what the author thinks? Give evidence from the article to support your ideas. Use your own piece of paper.

Prewriting
The author's purpose for writing the article is to:
The author presents information in the following order:
The author presents the following facts in the timeline:
These words and phrases help me identify ideas the author thinks are important:

Be sure to—

1. analyze how the structure of the article helps you understand the author's purpose.

2. explain how the author's word choices help you determine the most important points.

3. indicate how the timeline contributes to the overall purpose of the article.

4. support your ideas with facts from the article that relate to the topic.

Informational Text • *Genre Practice*

The Wolf in Sheep's Clothing

Read the passage below. Then answer the questions that follow.

Every day a hungry wolf spied on a flock of sheep as they grazed in a large pasture, trying to think of clever ways to catch one for his dinner. One hot afternoon he waited for hours behind a big rock, ready to pounce on the first sheep that wandered by. But when he heard something coming and jumped out of his hiding place, it wasn't a sheep at all. It was the shepherd and his sheepdog, who quickly chased the wolf away. The wolf began to think he would never outsmart the shepherd and his dog.

Then one day while he was wandering along a country road near the sheep pasture, the wolf found a bulky sheepskin rug that had fallen off the back of a delivery truck. "Ha!" he thought to himself. "I know what I'll do! I'll use this rug to disguise myself as a sheep. Then I'll easily be able to blend into the flock, and once I'm there. . . ." He began smacking his lips, thinking about the delicious mutton stew he'd have for his dinner that night.

The wolf dressed himself up in the sheepskin rug and trotted toward the sheep pasture. Along the way, he practiced talking in sheep language just in case he needed to fool the shepherd and his dog. "Baa-baa-grrr . . . baa-grr .... Baa-baa-grr." He had a hard time of it at first, but by the time he reached the pasture he was an expert in speaking sheep.

When the wolf reached the pasture, he found the sheep grazing contentedly. He slipped into the pasture, right beside a fat sheep who was nibbling a dandelion. The wolf thought he'd better nibble a bit too, just to blend in a little better, so he took a big chomp and gobbled up a dandelion in one bite. "Yuck!" he thought to himself. "But it'll all be worth it when I get my mutton stew tonight! At sunset the shepherd will herd us all into the pen, and when I'm tucked up tight with them I'll pick the fattest one."

The wolf mingled with the flock all day long, and the sheep didn't seem to pay him any mind, even though he was much bigger than any of them. Every so often he bleated out "Baa! Baa!" just to keep up appearances.

At sunset, the shepherd and his sheepdog herded the sheep into their pen, and in went the wolf with the rest of the flock. His disguise had worked! Not even the shepherd had noticed!

Suddenly, the sheepdog perked up his ears and sniffed the air. He looked up at the shepherd, then back toward the flock. The shepherd looked at the flock carefully, then he smiled and reached down to pat his dog's head.

"You know what, boy?" the shepherd began. "You've been working hard and I think you deserve something special for your dinner tonight. How about that great big sheep over there?" And before the wolf knew it, the shepherd reached out caught him around the neck with his shepherd's hook.

"Oh no!" thought the wolf. "I thought I was going to have a special dinner tonight, but it looks like I'M the dinner instead!" He wiggled and squirmed and freed himself from the shepherd's hook—but not before the sheepdog took several big bites out of him. Then he shot off fast as lightning out of the pen and as far away as his legs could carry him.

Fable • *Genre Practice*

Respond to Reading

Read each question. Circle the letter next to your answer choice.

1. What is one way you know this story is a fable?

   a. The story setting is a real place or could be a real place.

   b. The story is about something that did not really happen.

   c. The story includes an animal that thinks and acts like a person.

   d. The story includes characters that the reader cares about.

2. Read the following excerpt.

   > Suddenly, the sheepdog perked up his ears and sniffed the air. He looked up at the shepherd, then back toward the flock. The shepherd looked at the flock carefully, then he smiled and reached down to pat his dog's head.

   Why did the shepherd smile and pat his dog's head?

   f. He was thanking the dog for helping herd the sheep into the pen.

   g. He knew the dog wanted one of the sheep for dinner.

   h. Thanks to the dog's help, he had spotted the wolf in the flock.

   j. He wanted the dog to chase the wolf out of the sheep pen.

3. Read the following excerpt.

   > When the wolf reached the pasture, he found the sheep grazing contentedly. He slipped into the pasture, right beside a fat sheep who was nibbling a dandelion.

   Based on the text, what does the word *contentedly* mean?

   a. in a happy and satisfied way   c. in an enthusiastic manner

   b. with great sorrow   d. at a very fast rate

4. What would be the best moral for this story?

   f. It is easy to hate what you do not have.

   g. Never underestimate your weakest foe.

   h. Nothing comes easy without hard work.

   j. Do not pretend to be what you are not.

Genre Practice • Fable

Reread the fable "The Wolf in Sheep's Clothing" on pages 21–22.

Think about the ways the wolf in the fable acts like a wolf, and the ways he acts like a person. What does it mean for a person to be a "wolf in sheep's clothing"? What does the wolf's behavior have to do with the lesson? Organize your ideas. Use the space below for prewriting.

Write about the relationship between the title of the fable and the lesson the fable teaches. Give evidence from the fable to support your ideas. Use your own paper.

Prewriting	
Ways the wolf acted like a wolf	*Ways the wolf acted like a person*

Be sure to—

1. analyze the relationship between the fable's title and lesson.

2. explain the meaning of the phrase "a wolf in sheep's clothing."

3. consider how the wolf's behavior relates to the fable's lesson.

4. include details from the story to support your ideas.

Fable • *Genre Practice*

Welsh Prince Madoc Sails to America

Read the passage below. Then answer the questions that follow.

This is a tale of a brave explorer that has long been told, an explorer who sailed to America hundreds of years before Christopher Columbus. This is the story of Prince Madoc.

Madoc is the youngest son of King Owain of Wales, who has nineteen children. Upon the king's death, a dispute breaks out. Who will succeed the king? The oldest son, Yorweth, cannot. Yorweth has a scar on his face, and an old Welsh tradition says no one can rule with a scarred face. So a younger brother seizes the crown, but only for a short time, for he is killed by David, his brother. David is cruel. As king, he kills Yorweth, imprisons another brother, and threatens the others with death if they attempt to unseat him.

David's brutality disgusts Madoc. Being civilized and peaceful, he wants no part of the fighting. Madoc decides to leave his family and his homeland, and search for a better life elsewhere.

Madoc gathers a crew of other adventurers and sails west in two ships, searching for a place where all can live in harmony. In time, Madoc finds a place—America. But to achieve harmony, he needs more than time; he needs courage and intelligence.

Upon their arrival in America, Madoc and his crew encounter two native tribes, one small and peaceful, another powerful and fierce. Madoc believes if the smaller tribe could conquer the larger one, peace would prevail. At first, the battle between the two tribes seems unfair; one army is much bigger than the other.

Madoc, though, is determined and clever. Using skill and intellect, he leads the smaller tribe to victory. To the surprise of the defeated larger tribe, Madoc then orders all prisoners to be set free and provides needed medicine to their sick king. Madoc's generosity is rewarded. The larger tribe agrees to live peacefully with the smaller one. Finally, Madoc has found his land of harmony.

Madoc's story, however, does not end there. Oh, no. While part of his crew remains in America, Madoc returns to Wales. There he shares his stories of adventure and his descriptions of a new, peaceful place. He persuades others, including one of his brothers, to join him in settling this new, beautiful land. Once again, Madoc gathers an expedition, and they all set sail to America, only to be heard from no more.

Did Madoc sail to America? Some believe that he and the other Welsh people did make it back to America and settled in the area that is now known as Mobile Bay, Alabama. Old stone forts similar in design to Welsh castles have been found along the Alabama River. Tales of one native tribe who spoke a language and used coracles, a type of boat, similar to the Welsh have been passed down through the ages. However, no evidence has been produced that shows beyond a shadow of a doubt that Madoc sailed to America. Even so, Prince Madoc's story of his search for a land where people could live together in peace endures today.

Respond to Reading

Read each question. Circle the letter next to your answer choice.

1. What two important qualities of a legend does this story have?

    a. It includes magical events and happens in a made-up place.

    b. It is set in the past and may or may not be true.

    c. It includes animals and teaches a lesson.

    d. It tells about battles and has a happy ending.

2. Read the following excerpt.

    > Upon the king's death, a dispute breaks out. Who will succeed the king? The oldest son, Yorweth, cannot. Yorweth has a scar on his face, and an old Welsh tradition says no one can rule with a scarred face. So a younger brother seizes the crown, but only for a short time, for he is killed by David, his brother.

    What does the word *succeed* mean?

    f. achieve a goal

    g. become famous

    h. come after in order

    j. take over as leader

3. Which event causes a problem for Madoc?

    a. King Owain's death

    b. Madoc's arrival in America

    c. the release of prisoners

    d. the use of coracles

4. Which sentence from the passage best relates to the theme of the story?

    f. Madoc is the youngest son of King Owain of Wales, who has nineteen children.

    g. But to achieve harmony, he needs more than time; he needs courage and intelligence.

    h. He persuades others, including one of his brothers, to join him in settling this new, beautiful land.

    j. Old stone forts similar in design to Welsh castles have been found along the Alabama River.

Reread the last paragraph of "Welsh Prince Madoc Sails to America" on page 26.

Think about how the second to last sentence connects to the other details in the selection. Organize your ideas by using the prewriting space below.

Write a response in which you explain why the author includes the following sentence in the last paragraph: "However, no evidence has been produced that shows beyond a shadow of a doubt that Madoc sailed to America." Give evidence from the selection to support your ideas. Use your own piece of paper.

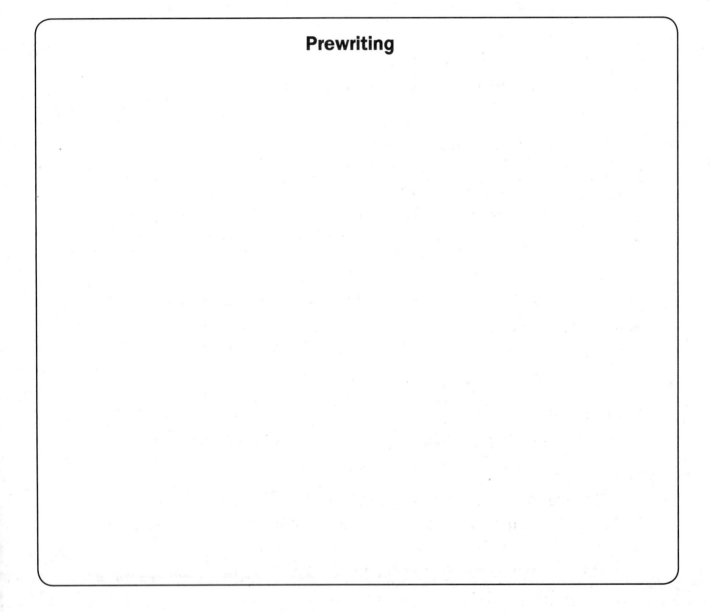

Prewriting

Be sure to—

1. explain why the sentence is included.

2. support your ideas with evidence from the passage.

3. connect ideas with linking words, such as *also, another,* and *but.*

4. use correct spelling, capitalization, punctuation, and grammar.

Legend • *Genre Practice*

The Golden Apple of Discord

Read the passage below. Then answer the questions that follow.

The wedding of King Peleus and the sea goddess Thetis was a grand event for mortals and gods alike. In fact, all the gods and goddess attended, all except one. Eris, the goddess of conflict, was not invited. This displeased her so much she decided to cause trouble by sneaking into the wedding and rolling a golden apple across the floor. The apple had the phrase "To the fairest" written on it. Such discord this apple caused as the goddesses Hera, Athena, and Aphrodite fought over it!

To stop the arguing, Zeus, the most powerful god, was called in to decide which goddess deserved the apple, who was the fairest. Zeus, being wise, knew that selecting one goddess would make the other two angry, so he turned to the mortal Paris, a prince of Troy, and told him to decide.

Each goddess thought she was the fairest. Each attempted to bribe Paris. Hera offered Paris a kingdom. Athena said she would make him the greatest warrior, and Aphrodite promised him the love of Helen, the most beautiful mortal woman. Paris accepted Aphrodite's offer and awarded her the golden apple.

In order to reach Helen, Paris had to sail to the city of Sparta in Greece. There, he found Helen, who fell madly in love with him, and the two returned to Troy. But the king of Sparta, King Menelaus, was not happy. He thought Helen had been kidnapped. Menelaus declared war and had his brother gather an army to attack Troy. Soon 1,000 ships sailed from Greece in order to rescue Helen.

When Menelaus's army arrived in Troy, a great battle began, a battle now known as the Trojan War. The war lasted for ten years, and many were killed, including Paris. But the Greeks were determined to find Helen.

Retrieving Helen was difficult because the city of Troy was surrounded by high rock walls. The Greeks could not get to her until one day, Odysseus, a Greek general, had a clever idea.

Odysseus ordered his men to build a great hollow wooden horse in which many soldiers could hide. As Odysseus and a few hundred soldiers hid in the horse, the remaining soldiers packed up everything in the camp—except the horse—and sailed away on their ships, only to hide in a cove nearby.

The Trojans, seeing the Greek ships leave and their camp deserted, thought the Greeks had given up and had offered the horse as a peace offering. They pushed the horse inside their city walls. The Trojans were joyful. At last, the long war was over. They celebrated their victory all day and into the night.

When the Trojans' celebration was over and all was quiet, Odysseus and his men quietly emerged from the horse and quickly opened the city gates to let in the other Greek soldiers, who had sailed back to Troy earlier in the night. With the Greeks now inside the city walls, they could defeat the Trojans and rescue Helen. And that's exactly what they did. Menelaus found Helen and took her back to Sparta.

Although the Greeks proved successful, many lives were lost during the Trojan War. Much suffering and grief was brought about, all for a golden apple.

Myth • *Genre Practice*

Respond to Reading

Read each question. Circle the letter next to your answer choice.

1. What about the characters shows you this passage is a myth?

    a. The good characters defeat evil ones.

    b. Some of the characters are gods.

    c. Many of the characters are warriors.

    d. The characters lived long ago.

2. Read the following excerpt.

    > Such *discord* this apple caused as the goddesses Hera, Athena, and Aphrodite fought over it!

    What is the meaning of *discord*?

    f. arguing   **h.** deciding

    g. powers   **j.** fairness

3. Which sentence helps the reader predict the Greeks will win the Trojan War?

    a. Menelaus declared war and had his brother gather an army to attack Troy.

    b. The war lasted for several years, and many were killed, including Paris.

    c. Retrieving Helen was difficult because high rock walls surrounded Troy.

    d. One day the Greek general Odysseus came up with a clever plan.

4. Which is the best summary of the passage?

    f. Eris was not invited. To cause trouble, she tossed in a golden apple that read, "To the fairest." When three goddesses claimed it, Zeus made Paris the judge.

    g. Eris's trick led to the Trojan War when Paris took Helen away. The Greeks won by sneaking into Troy in a wooden horse. Paris died and Helen returned home.

    h. Eris's golden apple caused three goddesses to fight. Paris was asked to stop the argument by choosing which goddess was the fairest. He chose Aphrodite. In return Aphrodite made Helen fall in love with Paris.

    j. Eris's anger at not being invited to a wedding caused the Trojan War. While the war lasted many years, the Greeks eventually won when they used a wooden horse to sneak into Troy.

Reread the last paragraph of "The Golden Apple of Discord" on page 30.

Think about the role the golden apple plays in the story. Organize your ideas. Use the space below for prewriting.

Write a response in which you explain why the story ends with a reference to the golden apple. Give evidence from the passage to support your ideas. Use your own piece of paper.

Prewriting

Be sure to—

1. explain why the golden apple is mentioned at the end of the story.

2. provide evidence from the passage.

3. use linking words, such as *also, another,* and *but.*

4. use correct spelling, capitalization, punctuation, and grammar.

Stopping School Bullying

Read both passages. Then answer the questions that follow.

Bullying is a serious problem in American schools, affecting up to 30 percent of all students. Bullying hurts both the bully and the target. Bullies often lack the social and emotional skills they need to get along with others. Difficult family situations frequently cause them to lash out at other students. Unless their problems are solved, many will have futures marked by school failure, depression, violence, and crime. Targets also face significant mental health risks: embarrassment, fear, anxiety, and powerlessness. In many cases, targets become bullies themselves.

Fortunately, schools are beginning to find ways to help these at-risk students and stamp out bullying. The No Bully System is an anti-bullying program teachers and administrators are using to resolve up to 90 percent of bullying in their schools.

The No Bully System is based on the belief that bullying situations happen mainly because students don't know how to deal with their personal challenges—not because students are "bad kids." The program helps students develop missing coping skills. One key element of the program is the use of Solution Teams—groups of student peers who work together to stop the bullying.

School staff bring together the team—which includes the bully and his or her friends, the target, and positive student leaders—to discuss the situation. No one is in trouble. Instead, the team discusses how both the bully and the target feel, allowing both to feel welcomed and heard. Student peers use the power of empathy to end the bullying and to provide reassurance to the target. Solution Teams are reducing bullying and helping targets feel safer. Everyone wins!

The Dog and His Reflection

There once was a dog who lived on a farm. He barked and snapped at the farmer and his wife, and every time he did they cried out, "Bad dog! What a bad dog!" So that became his name: Bad Dog.

At dinnertime, the farmer prepared a big bowl of meat and gravy and other delicious morsels for each dog, but Bad Dog always ran to the bowls first. He snarled and growled and turned up his lips to show the other dogs how sharp his teeth were. Then Bad Dog ate all the best bits out of the other dogs' bowls. The other dogs were afraid of Bad Dog, so they never tried to stop him.

One afternoon, Bad Dog smelled something wonderful coming from the farmhouse kitchen. He peeked in the window and saw a big, juicy roast on the table. Bad Dog jumped through the window, grabbed the roast in his jaws, and ran away with it. He heard the farmer's wife screaming at him in the distance as he ran down the road with his prize.

Bad Dog ran until he came to a little bridge. He thought this would be a good place to stop and eat the roast he'd stolen. But when he looked over the side of the bridge into the water below, he saw another dog—and this dog had a big, juicy roast in his mouth too!

Bad Dog had to have it. He opened his mouth to snarl and growl at the other dog . . . and the roast fell out of his mouth into the water and was swept away. Bad Dog had seen his own reflection, and now instead of two roasts, he had none.

Respond to Reading

Read each question. Circle the letter next to your answer choice.

1. The purpose of the passage "Stopping School Bullying" is to—
   a. inform readers about an anti-bullying program.
   b. persuade schools to use the No Bully System.
   c. entertain students with a story about school bullies.
   d. convince readers bullies should be punished.

2. Which idea is supported by the first paragraph of "Stopping School Bullying"?
   f. Students who are targeted by bullies suffer more than the bullies themselves.
   g. Swift punishment is the best way to combat school bullying.
   h. Both bullies and their targets often have emotional problems.
   j. Bullying is just a phase that most kids go through.

3. "The Dog and His Reflection" is considered a fable because it—
   a. is about a farm and the animals that live there.
   b. has a moral and animal characters with human characteristics.
   c. is based on events that occurred a long time ago.
   d. contains facts that can be verified in an online encyclopedia.

4. In "The Dog and His Reflection," the details in the first paragraph help explain—
   f. why Bad Dog runs away from the farm.
   g. how Bad Dog loses the roast.
   h. why the other dogs are afraid of Bad Dog.
   j. how Bad Dog gets his name.

5. What is one way the two selections are similar?

    a. They are both intended to amuse the reader.

    b. They both are meant to be read aloud.

    c. They both address the same topic.

    d. They are both organized in chronological order.

6. What is one difference between the two selections?

    f. One is about an issue people face, and the other is about an issue animals face.

    g. One is meant to entertain and the other is intended to persuade.

    h. One is written to be read and the other is written to be acted out in front of an audience.

    j. One is meant to provide information and the other is intended to teach a lesson.

7. Which idea is found in both selections?

    a. Bullying hurts both the bully and the ones being bullied.

    b. Bullies are always stronger than their targets.

    c. The best way to end bullying is for targets to fight back.

    d. It is very satisfying when a bully gets a deserved punishment.

8. Which idea is found in only one of the selections?

    f. Sometimes bullies behave badly because they have been told they are bad.

    g. Even those who bully can learn to behave kindly when they feel supported.

    h. The targets of bullies are often afraid to fight back.

    j. Bullies usually grow out of their behavior when they are older.

Comparing Genres • *Genre Practice*

Name _____ **Date** _____

Comparing Genres

Reread the passages "Stopping School Bullying" and "The Dog and His Reflection" on pages 33–34.

Think about each author's purpose. What does each author want you to think about bullying when you finish reading? Do the authors seem to feel the same way toward bullies? How do you know? Organize your ideas. Use the space below for prewriting.

Write about how the authors of each passage talk about bullies in different ways and for different purposes. Give evidence from the passages to support your ideas. Use your own paper for this writing assignment.

Prewriting		
	"Stopping School Bullying"	"The Dog and His Reflection"
What kind of passage is this? How do you know?		
Why did the author write this passage?		
What kinds of words does the author use to describe bullies? How does this tell you what the author thinks about bullies?		
What does the author want you to feel at the end of the passage? How do the author's words help you feel this way?		

Be sure to—

1. include the topic or topics you are comparing.

2. use clue words for comparing such as *also, like,* and *too.*

3. use clue words for contrasting such as *but, however,* and *although.*

4. conclude with a summary of your main points.

Revising

Use this checklist to revise your writing.

- Does your writing have a clear purpose?

- Does your writing compare and contrast the two passages?

- Does your writing have evidence to support your ideas?

- Does your writing include interesting details or descriptions?

- Did you include an ending that sums up your comparison?

Editing/Proofreading

Use this checklist to correct mistakes in your writing.

- Did you use proofreading symbols when editing?

- Does your writing include transition words?

- Did you check for subject/verb agreement?

- Did you check your writing for spelling mistakes?

Publishing

Use this checklist to prepare your writing for publishing.

- Write or type a neat copy of your writing.

- Add a photograph or a drawing.

The Long Life of Roman Roads

Read the passage below. Then answer the questions that follow.

Do all roads lead to Rome? At one time, they did. During the Roman Empire, Romans constructed a network of roads that covered fifty thousand miles, connecting the capital city of Rome to other territories in the empire. The Romans were skilled engineers. In fact, some of the roads they constructed more than two thousand years ago can still be seen today.

When the Romans conquered a region, the army built roads to connect that region to Rome. The roads had many purposes. They allowed the Roman army to move quickly to places where there was trouble. They also served as a way for people within the empire to trade and communicate with one another.

Roman roads were made from a variety of materials—whatever the army could find—but they were almost always straight. The Romans built their roads for speed and knew the shortest distance between two points is a straight line. To that end, the Romans planned their roads carefully. They used an instrument called a *groma* to lay out the straight lines. After they had a route planned, soldiers prepared the road's foundation. They dug a trench and filled it with small stones and sand. Next, they added a layer of cemented crushed gravel or brick. When they completed the foundation, they arranged large blocks of volcanic rock, cobbles, or stone on top, creating a flat surface on which carts could easily travel.

The Roman roads were not completely flat though. The Romans purposefully designed their roads so the middle was slightly higher than the sides. This incline discouraged rainwater from pooling in a road and flooding it. Instead, the water ran off to the sides and collected in ditches along both sides of the road.

In some ways the Roman network of roads was similar to our modern-day roadway system. Their major roads were much like our interstate highways. Roman soldiers constructed roads to move traffic quickly and efficiently. For example, soldiers built frequently traveled Roman roads wide enough so two chariots could pass each other. In addition, these roads had places where travelers could pull over and rest or restock supplies, much like the rest areas we have today. And just as we use road signs and mile markers to guide us on our trips, Roman travelers used them too.

While many Roman roads were neglected and went to ruin after the fall of the Roman Empire, some original sections remain. In fact, part of the Appian Way, a major Roman road, is now used as a walking and biking path in Rome. It serves as proof of the care the Romans took in building their roads. But the Romans also took care in planning their roads, and fortunately their plans were put to good use. Many of the routes the Romans planned served as guides for modern highways. For example, the Fosse Way carried people from the southwest of England to the northwest. The original road is gone, but new ones have been built along the route, so travelers today can make the same trip the ancient Romans made. The Romans were remarkable engineers. They planned and built their roads to last, and they did.

Writing to Sources • *Genre Practice*

Respond to Reading

Read each question, then write your answers on the lines. For questions that ask you to underline text evidence, mark your evidence on the pages 39–40.

1. According to the selection, why did the Romans build roads?

   _____

   _____

   _____

2. What is a *groma*? Why was it important to the Romans?

   _____

   _____

   _____

3. According to the selection, how did the Romans build their roads? Paraphrase the steps in order.

   _____

   _____

   _____

4. How did the Romans prevent their roads from flooding? Underline the text that provides this information.

   _____

   _____

   _____

5. According to the selection, how are Roman roads used today?

_____

_____

_____

6. Compare Roman roads to modern roads. In what ways are they similar? How are they different?

_____

_____

_____

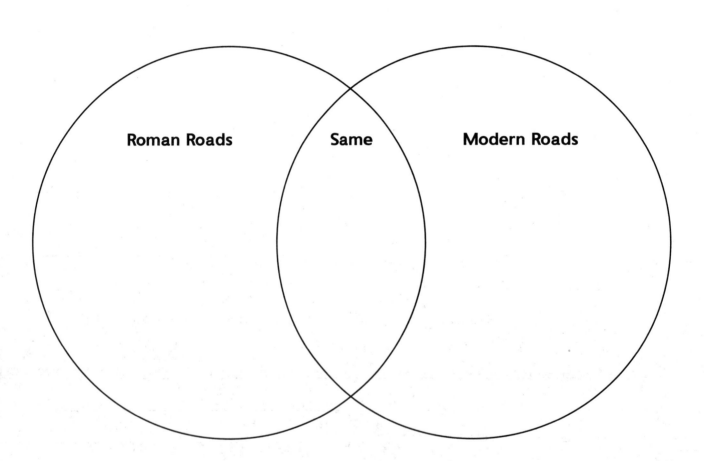

Writing to Sources • *Genre Practice*

Name _____ **Date** _____

The Princess and the Boggun

Read the passage below. Then answer the questions that follow.

"What are you doing here, girl?" The rumbling voice of a boggun was unmistakable. "Everything east of Glistening Creek belongs to us! Even a human should know that!"

The girl turned her head in time to see the tall, stout creature emerge from behind a tree. Two small eyes examined her closely from their deep sockets. Short, bent ears sat on each side of a long, pointy head covered in coarse black hair. Lips curled in a snarl, the creature opened his mouth to speak again before she cut him off.

"I am Kira, princess of Dusembia," the girl exclaimed proudly, tossing her wild red hair, emerald eyes blazing. "And our dominion extends to the Forest of Krad . . . as you well know, boggun!" She raised her sword menacingly. "That's where the likes of you belong . . . so get back to the dark woods where your kind dwell."

"I have a name!" the boggun growled as he reached into his cloak, "and my own weapon as well." He brandished a dagger, steel blade glistening in the sun, before tossing it aside. "But Vivort needs no weapon to remove a puny girl from his territory . . . princess or not! If you think you're going to steal more land from us, you're mistaken!"

As Vivort took a step toward Kira, her sword began to flash. "One touch of my blade, boggun, and you'll be transported to the Lost Maze, whence none have ever escaped." Vivort stopped abruptly, and Kira glared at him. "That's right. . . I see you have no wish to visit there."

Before Vivort could answer, a shrill screech pierced the air. He and Kira looked up to see a dragon swooping toward them, beak snapping and thorny claws open to snatch them both. They dashed toward a nearby row of bushes and dived in together, narrowly avoiding the dragon's talons. The monster shrieked in anger and circled in the air to make another attack.

"Dragons are relentless!" Vivort yelled above the dragon's caws. "It won't stop until it's made a meal of one of us . . . or both of us!"

"Then we'll need to work together somehow," Kira answered. "I'll grant that bogguns have a reputation for bravery. . . ."

"Indeed!" Vivort retorted, eyeing the winged lizard, which was preparing for another strike. "You have a plan?"

Kira looked hard at Vivort. "You'll need to trust me . . . and my sword." He nodded, and Kira smiled admiringly. "Then move out into the open—just beside those bushes." She gestured with her weapon, and understanding her plan, Vivort scrambled from his hiding place. He stood tall and proud, shaking his fist defiantly at the dragon.

"Do you dare attack a boggun?" Vivort bellowed. "Here I am—see whether you can catch me!" The dragon flapped its leathery wings, hovering in the air and blinking its savage amber eyes at Vivort before hurtling toward him. Vivort glanced toward the bushes, where Kira crouched, sword at the ready.

Just as the dragon extended its claws to seize Vivort, Kira sprang from the bushes and swung her sword, which crashed against the dragon's belly. Instantly, the monster was carried away to the Lost Maze.

Panting breathlessly, Kira and Vivort regarded each other with gratitude and newfound respect.

"My subjects and I are indebted, Vivort."

"And I am beholden as well . . . princess."

The two reached out to join hands. "Perhaps both of us can use the land between creek and forest," said Kira.

"Perhaps so," Vivort answered with a smile.

Respond to Reading

Read each question. Circle the letter next to your answer choice.

1. How can the reader identify this selection as fantasy?

   a. One of the main characters is a princess.

   b. The story takes place at some time in the recent past.

   c. It uses imagination to draw the reader into the story.

   d. Things happen that could not happen in the real world.

2. The conversation between Kira and Vivort at the end of the story shows that—

   f. humans and boggarts have very different feelings about dragons.

   g. their encounter with the dragon has formed the basis of a friendship.

   h. Vivort is willing to give the Forest of Krad to Kira and her people.

   j. they do not intend to tell anyone else about their fight with the dragon.

3. Reread the third paragraph on page 43. Based on the text, which word is most closely related to the word *dominion*?

   a. dominate

   b. domestic

   c. domino

   d. domed

4. How does the author use the setting to help establish the relationship between Kira and Vivort at the beginning of the story?

   f. Vivort wants to become ruler of Dusembia, which angers Kira.

   g. The mysterious surroundings show that Kira is keeping a secret from Vivort.

   h. Kira and Vivort dislike each other because they both claim the same territory.

   j. Kira is frightened of the Forest of Krad, which makes Vivort believe she is weak.

Reread the passage "The Princess and the Boggun" on pages 43–44.

Think about the words the author uses to talk about the characters. Why does the author describe the characters like this? What does the author want you to think about them? Organize your ideas. Use the space below for prewriting.

Write about the ways the author describes Kira, Vivort, and the dragon. How do these descriptions help you understand the characters and their personalities? Give evidence from the article to support your ideas. Include a picture of one of the characters using the description in the story. Write on a separate piece of paper.

Prewriting			
	Kira	**Vivort**	**The Dragon**
Words the author uses to describe the character's <u>appearance</u>			
Words the author uses to describe the character's <u>words</u> and <u>actions</u>			
Words you would use to describe the character			

Be sure to—

1. examine the way the author describes the characters and what that tells you about their personalities.

2. analyze how the author's word choices paint a mental picture of the characters for the reader.

3. support your ideas with facts from the story that relate to the topic.

4. include a drawing of one of the characters based on the descriptions in the story.

5. proofread, revise, and edit your writing as needed to improve clarity and eliminate mistakes.

Fantasy • *Genre Practice*

Career Choice: By Passion or Practicality?

Read the passage below. Then answer the questions that follow.

There comes a time in your life when you must decide what you want to do for a living. When making this decision, one key question comes to mind. Do you follow your heart and choose a career based on what you love, or do you follow your head and choose a career that pays the bills? It's a tough question, one that requires a cool head, because your head knows it makes more sense to choose a practical career.

Some may argue you should do what you love. A job you're passionate about will motivate you, which in turn leads to success. Look at Neil Armstrong, for example. At age six, Armstrong took his first airplane ride. This event affected him so strongly that Armstrong decided to pursue a career in aviation. He studied aeronautical engineering. He served as a pilot during the Korean War. After the war, he was a research pilot, testing different types of planes. He eventually worked for NASA, where he had the honor of being the pilot of the first spacecraft to land on the moon. Armstrong's passion for flying is evident throughout his career.

Not everyone can follow a path like Neil Armstrong though. It's important to note NASA hires fewer than twenty astronauts every two years, yet they receive an average of thirty-five hundred applications. The chances of someone who has a passion for space or space travel becoming an astronaut are slim. The same is true for those who have a passion for baseball or ballet. Unfortunately, all those people cannot be professional players or dancers. There just aren't enough openings. The opportunities to make money by doing something you love may be limited. Therefore, it's important to select a more practical career.

Practical jobs, such as teacher, doctor, plumber, accountant, and electrician, are ones society regularly needs. Go to any city or town, and you will find people doing these jobs. Having a job that is needed and is available in most places provides a degree of stability. In other words, people with practical jobs are able to find jobs more easily, which means they are able to make money and provide for their families.

Seeking a practical career doesn't mean you have to give up your passion. In fact, the money you make from having a practical job can help you do what you love outside of work. And keeping your passion separate from your job is often a good idea. Some people have found that when they turn a passion into a career, they ruin what they love. Imagine someone who loves to bake. Every opportunity she gets, she bakes bread for friends and family. This same person then decides to open a bakery. Now, instead of baking two to three loaves of bread every week, the baker has to make hundreds. Instead of baking a few hours every once in a while, the baker has to bake every day. Instead of baking on her terms, the baker now has to cope with customers, suppliers, and employees. For this person, baking is no longer fun. It's work.

"Follow your heart" might seem like good advice when selecting a career, but using your head is better advice. A practical career offers more options and more stability. Having a practical job doesn't mean you can't pursue your passions. In fact, having both—a practical job and something you love—is an ideal option.

Argumentative Text • *Genre Practice*

Respond to Reading

Read each question. Circle the letter next to your answer choice.

1. The author most likely wrote this passage to—
    a. explain how to do something.
    b. describe the events in a person's life.
    c. convince readers that an idea is true.
    d. provide a solution to a problem.

2. Read the following sentence.

    > It's important to note NASA hires fewer than twenty astronauts every two years, yet they receive on average thirty-five hundred applications.

    The author most likely includes this sentence to—
    f. support the idea that finding a job based on a passion may be difficult.
    g. highlight Neil Armstrong's achievements as an astronaut.
    h. explain the process NASA uses to hire new astronauts.
    j. provide a reason why getting a job based on a passion is often rewarding.

3. What is the fourth paragraph mainly about?
    a. how difficult it is to find a job in a new city
    b. why having a practical job and a passion are important
    c. why jobs based on a passion are needed
    d. how practical jobs offer people more opportunities to work

4. Which sentence from the passage best expresses the author's main idea?
    f. There comes a time in your life when you must decide what you want to do for a living.
    g. Armstrong's passion for flying is evident throughout his career.
    h. Therefore, it's important to select a more practical career.
    j. Every opportunity she gets, she bakes bread for friends and family.

Reread the final paragraph of the passage on page 48 to find the author's conclusion.

Think about reasons for and against the author's argument. Did the author change your mind? How could the author have strengthened the argument? Organize your ideas. Use the space below for prewriting.

Write an essay explaining whether the author of the passage convinced you to consider a practical career. Use specific examples from the selection. Write your essay on your own piece of paper.

For a Practical Career	Against a Practical Career

Be sure to—

1. explain if you choose a career based on passion or practicality.

2. support your ideas with evidence from the passage.

3. use linking words, such as *also*, *another*, and *but*.

4. use correct spelling, capitalization, punctuation, and grammar.

The Snow Maiden

Read the passage below. Then answer the questions that follow.

A long time ago in a village near the woods lived an old peasant and his wife. The two were happy but had one regret—they had no children of their own.

It came to pass one winter day that the snow fell heavily and piled so high that everyone stayed indoors. When the sun finally appeared, the village children took to the streets to build forts and people made out of snow. From their window, the peasant and his wife watched the children playing happily.

"Masha," the husband called to his wife, "why don't we build a little girl with all this snow?"

After being stuck inside all day, Masha decided it would be fun to join the merriment outside. "Yes, Akem," she replied, "Let's build a snow child. We can pretend it is ours."

Masha and Akem shaped the snow into a child. After they built the snow child's body, Akem placed a snowball on top to serve as a head. He first drew the eyes, then a nose, and finally a mouth. As he was finishing, a warm breath came out of the snow child's mouth. Akem was surprised. He bent down and peered closely at the snow child's head. Where he had drawn eyes, he now saw eyes as blue as the sky. Where he had drawn a curve for a mouth, he saw lips as red as raspberries.

"What is this?" Akem shouted. As he and Masha watched, the snow child's head, arms, and legs began to move, shaking the snow away to reveal a real, living girl.

The couple ran to the girl, threw their arms around her, and covered her with kisses. "Oh, Akem," cried Masha. "We have a child, our own little Snow Maiden!"

As the winter months went on, the Snow Maiden grew tall and beautiful. She was lively and kind, bringing much joy to her parents and making many friends.

Soon, though, spring approached. The grass grew high, and the flowers bloomed, but as the days got brighter, the Snow Maiden's mood grew darker. She hid away in the shadows and no longer played with her friends. Only in the cool nights or during a dark storm would her good nature return.

The Snow Maiden's friends left her alone until the day of the summer festival. Then they went to her and begged her to join them. Masha thought time with her daughter's friends might cheer her, and so she said, "Go, Snow Maiden, and play with your friends. And to you, friends, please take care of her for she means the world to me."

The children set off to the forest, singing and dancing together all day. When the sun set, they gathered around the festival fire. The children huddled closely together so they could tell each other stories. As the children shared their tales, some of the villagers attending the festival threw more wood on the fire. Big flames burst from the fire, and a wave of heat rushed over all the children as they turned to watch vibrant colors dance against the night sky.

Suddenly, they heard a scream. The children looked back and did not see the Snow Maiden. At first, the children thought she might be hiding for fun, but when they could not find her, they thought she had run home.

The Snow Maiden had not gone home, and when Akem and Masha learned she was missing, they were heartbroken. For four days and nights, they searched for her. Masha called, "My dear Snow Maiden, where are you?" But she never received an answer. What had become of the Snow Maiden? Had a wild animal dragged her away? Had a bird carried her off?

No, neither beast nor bird took the Snow Maiden. It was the fire. When the burst of hot air blew past the children, she melted away, leaving behind a little cloud that drifted up toward the sky.

Respond to Reading

Read each question. Circle the letter next to your answer choice.

1. The story of the Snow Maiden best explains—
   a. the changing of the seasons.
   b. how children played in the past.
   c. the power of friendship.
   d. how winter can be harsh.

2. Read the following excerpt.

   > Where he had drawn eyes, he now saw eyes as blue as the sky. Where he had drawn a curve for a mouth, he saw lips as red as raspberries.

   What feeling do you get from the author's use of similes?
   f. hunger
   g. satisfaction
   h. terror
   j. excitement

3. Why does the Snow Maiden stop playing with her friends?
   a. She believes the children dislike her.
   b. She does not understand the games they play.
   c. She does not want to play outside in the sun.
   d. She prefers to stay with her parents.

4. What is the main theme of the story?
   f. Happiness can disappear in an instant, so we should enjoy it when we find it.
   g. Children bring happiness to their parents.
   h. People who work hard often achieve their dreams.
   j. Kindness leads to friendship.

Reread the first two paragraphs on page 52.

Think about how the Snow Maiden changes and the words and phrases the author uses to describe this change. Organize your ideas. Use the chart below for prewriting.

Write a response in which you explain how the author's words relate to a change in the Snow Maiden. Give evidence from the reading selection to support your ideas. Write your response on a separate sheet of paper.

Words and Phrases Describing the Snow Maiden in Winter	Words and Phrases Describing the Snow Maiden in Spring

Be sure to—

1. explain how the author's words show how the Snow Maiden changes.

2. support your ideas with evidence from the reading selection.

3. connect your ideas with linking words, such as *also, another,* and *but.*

4. use correct spelling, capitalization, punctuation, and grammar.

Margaret E. Knight: The "Lady Edison"

Read the passage below. Then answer the questions that follow.

Born in Maine in 1838, Margaret E. Knight always had a knack for inventing. Instead of playing with dolls, Knight enjoyed making things with woodworking tools.

"I couldn't see the sense in coddling bits of porcelain with senseless faces," she later explained. "I was fascinated with jackknives, wood, and tools." Knight used her father's toolbox and a sketchbook she labeled My Inventions to make toys, kites, and sleds for her brothers and a foot warmer for her mother. It seemed Knight could invent almost anything if she put her mind to it!

After Knight's father died when she was still very young, her brothers found jobs at a textile mill in New Hampshire. Sometimes Knight visited her brothers at the mill. During one of those visits, she saw something dreadful. One of the fabric-weaving looms malfunctioned, and a sharp, steel-tipped shuttle broke off. The piece flew from the machine, hitting and badly injuring a mill worker.

Knight's Paper Bag

You might have used Margaret Knight's most famous invention at lunchtime today without even knowing it! In 1870 she invented a machine that made the first flat-bottomed paper bag. When a machine-shop worker stole her design and tried to patent the device, Knight had to prove in court she was the rightful inventor. (One of the machine-shop worker's arguments was that a woman could not possibly invent such a complicated machine.) Knight won the case and received a patent for her device. She went on to establish her own company, the Eastern Paper Bag Company. Today, more than seven thousand machines around the world produce the same kind of flat-bottomed paper bags Knight designed almost one hundred fifty years ago.

The incident at the mill motivated Knight to invent a device that would prevent such accidents. Although many people had been trying to find a way to make the looms safer, none of their ideas had worked. But Knight was determined! Soon she had invented a simple stop-motion safety device that held the shuttles in place and turned off the entire machine if something went wrong. Knight was only twelve years old when she invented her device. Her invention soon became a standard part on all looms and made textile mills much safer.

Unfortunately, Knight did not earn a single dollar for her invention. She and her family did not think to patent the safety device. (A *patent* is a right granted to an inventor that prevents others from using or selling the invention without permission.) Plus, in the mid-nineteenth century, women and girls were not encouraged to file patents. But this is not the end of Knight's story.

During her lifetime Knight invented and patented many other machines and devices, such as a numbering machine, a window frame and sash, and several parts for automobile engines. She was such a prolific inventor she became known as the "Lady Edison." Knight's inventions did not make her wealthy, but her creative genius continues to inspire.

Name _____ Date _____

Respond to Reading

Read each question. Circle the letter next to your answer choice.

1. How do you know this article is an example of informational text?

   a. One of the main characters in the article is a "lady inventor."

   b. The article tells about things Margaret Knight actually accomplished.

   c. The author wants to persuade girls to become inventors like Margaret Knight.

   d. The article describes things that occurred more than a hundred years ago.

2. The author includes a sidebar in the article about Margaret Knight to—

   f. give more evidence that Knight's inventions saved lives.

   g. reinforce the claim in the story that Knight invented many helpful machines and devices.

   h. show people still use Knight's inventions today.

   j. illustrate how important it is for inventors to obtain patents.

3. Read the following excerpt from the passage.

   > During one of those visits, she saw something dreadful. One of the fabric-weaving looms malfunctioned and a sharp, steel-tipped shuttle broke off. The piece flew from the machine, hitting and badly injuring a mill worker.

   Based on the text, which word is a synonym for *dreadful*?

   a. unique   **c.** surprising

   b. exciting   **d.** horrible

4. What is the best summary of this selection?

   f. Thanks to Margaret Knight, many mill workers' lives were saved after her invention became widely used.

   g. If Margaret Knight had patented all her inventions, she would have become a wealthy woman.

   h. Clever from a young age, Margaret Knight designed many important devices at a time when women did not often work as inventors.

   j. More women should pursue careers in science and technology, like Margaret Knight did.

Reread "Margaret Knight: The Lady Edison" on pages 55–56.

Think about the events in the selection. Why does the author describe events in sequential order? What does the author want you to understand? Does this structure make it easy or hard for you to follow along with the selection? Organize your ideas. Use the space below for prewriting.

Write about the way the author organizes the facts about Margaret Knight. Why does the author organize the text like this? How does this organization support the author's purpose? Give evidence from the article to support your ideas. Write on a separate sheet of paper.

Prewriting
What happens in the first paragraph?
What happens in the second paragraph?
What happens in the third paragraph?
What happens in the fourth paragraph?

Be sure to—

1. describe the way the author organizes the facts in the article.

2. explain how writing in sequential order supports the author's purpose.

3. support your ideas with facts from the article that relate to the topic.

4. proofread, revise, and edit your writing as needed to improve clarity and eliminate mistakes.

Informational Text • *Genre Practice*

Name _____ **Date** _____

King Log and King Stork

Read the passage below. Then answer the questions that follow.

No one ever understood why the frogs were so unhappy. It was summertime—their favorite time of year—and they should have been content to splash around peacefully in their pond and catch flies. Yes, they should have been quite satisfied. But they were not.

"I'm sooooo bored," croaked a great big bullfrog.

"I am too," answered a shiny green frog. "All we do is eat and swim, eat and swim, maybe hop around from one lily pad to another. We need some more excitement in this pond!"

"Well now, what we really need . . . is a king," cried the bullfrog. "Just imagine! Our very own king with a great crown of gold, entertaining us all day with the pomp and display of royalty. He could give us orders and keep us busy all day long."

The other frogs quickly agreed and, filled with excitement, they called out to the great god Jupiter to send them a king.

Jupiter laughed to himself at the foolish creatures, who really did have all they needed. To keep them quiet, he cast a large log into their pond, saying, "Behold! Here is the King of Frogs!"

At first, the frogs were frightened of the huge log and hid among the reeds and grasses surrounding the pond. After a while, though, some of the braver frogs ventured out and began to swim closer to their enormous king, waiting for him to issue his first command. But the new king just floated on his back, never saying a word.

"Bit quiet, isn't he," said the shiny green frog, "for a king?"

The others agreed.

Days and days passed, and the king never seemed to move, so after a while the frogs stopped thinking of him as a king altogether. The younger frogs began using him as a diving platform, while the older frogs stretched out on him to sunbathe and complain about what a bad king Jupiter had sent them. They deserved a proper king who moved around, being powerful and strong and telling them what to do—not this docile creature.

Now Jupiter was listening to all this, and the noisy, ungrateful frogs were making him very angry indeed. So he lifted his right hand.

"You frogs want a powerful king?" he shouted. "Let's see how you like this one!" And from out of the sky swooped a huge white stork, the biggest any of the frogs had ever seen. The terrified frogs hopped this way and that as the stork began gobbling them up in his huge beak. Soon they realized how foolish they had been.

"Please, mighty Jupiter!" the bullfrog croaked desperately. "Take away this cruel tyrant before we are all destroyed!" But Jupiter only laughed scornfully.

"Are you still not satisfied? You have what you asked for, so you have only yourselves to blame for your misfortunes."

But none of the frogs answered him—they had all disappeared.

Respond to Reading

Read each question. Circle the letter next to your answer choice.

1. Which characteristic of a fable is found in this story?

   a. One character is a god.

   b. The story includes magic.

   c. One character is a king.

   d. The story teaches a lesson.

2. What made the frogs think the log was not a good king?

   f. The log was sent by Jupiter.

   g. The log was not assertive.

   h. The log floated in the pond.

   j. The log could not croak like a frog.

3. Reread the first paragraph on page 60. What is the meaning of the word *docile*?

   a. foolish

   b. timid

   c. proud

   d. wise

4. What would be the best moral for this story?

   f. Be sure you can better your condition before you try to change it.

   g. Do not let pride make you overestimate your powers.

   h. Behavior that is acceptable in one is very rude in another.

   j. Do not play tricks on your friends unless you can stand to be tricked yourself.

Reread the story "King Log and King Stork" on pages 59–60.

Think about what makes a story a fable. Which characteristics of a fable does the author use? What features make this story a fable and not some other genre, like a tall tale or a myth? Organize your ideas. Use the space below for prewriting.

Write about the how the author uses the characteristics of a fable to write this story. Convince the reader this story is a fable and not some other type of story. Give evidence from the article to support your ideas. Use your own paper or a paper provided by your teacher.

Prewriting	
Characteristics of a Fable	**Example from the Story**

Be sure to—

1. describe the characteristics of a fable and explain how each is used in the story.

2. explain what makes this story a fable and not some other genre.

3. state your claim, and support it with facts from the story that relate to the topic.

4. proofread, revise, and edit your writing as needed to improve clarity and eliminate mistakes.

Fable • *Genre Practice*

Letter to a Professional Athlete

Read the passage below. Then answer the questions that follow.

June 3, 2018

Tiana Lewis
256 Ferndale Drive
San Diego, CA 92027

Dear Ms. Lewis:

Congratulations on your second-place finish in the Challenge Xtreme triathlon. I watched the race on television and was amazed by your performance. Swimming in the ocean for more than two miles, then biking 112 miles, finally running a 26-mile marathon must be exhausting, but you were able to complete the grueling course and set a personal best time. You inspire me, so I'm writing to learn more about you.

You see, I am a triathlete too. My family has three triathletes—my brother, my mom, and me. My mother and I became interested in triathlons after watching my brother compete in one. Now, we often compete together as a team in short triathlons. My mother swims; I bike; and my brother runs. How did you become interested in triathlons?

Currently, I'm training for my first individual race, which will take place in August. Of course, it's not a long-distance one like the Challenge Xtreme. For my triathlon, I will swim one hundred fifty meters, bike for four miles, and run for under two miles. I train four days a week, one hour each day. On Tuesday, I practice swimming; on Wednesday, I practice biking; on Friday, I practice running, and on Saturday, I do mini races. I always make sure two of my practices include intervals where I swim, bike, or run as fast as I can repeatedly over short distances. What is your training schedule? Do you practice one sport each day like I do? How often do you do intervals?

I'm both excited and nervous about the triathlon in August, because it will be the first one where I participate in all three sports. I'm not concerned about the biking and running segments, but the swimming portion is another story. I don't mind swimming in a pool, but for this triathlon, I'll have to swim in a lake. Swimming with fish doesn't bother me. It's getting tangled in *Hydrilla,* those longs weeds that grow underwater, that is worrisome because it throws off my cadence, the rhythm of my swim strokes. Do you have a least favorite section of the triathlon? If so, what do you do to build up your confidence?

At the end of the Challenge Xtreme, a reporter asked if you were disappointed you came in second place. You said you weren't because you think a triathlon is more of a competition with yourself rather than one with other people, and because you had set a new personal best, you were pleased with your finish. You went on to say that winning is not the goal of all the training you do. Instead, the goal is being proud of what you've accomplished. I appreciated your answer. As I prepare for my first full triathlon, do you have any other advice that will keep me motivated?

Thank you for your time in reading my letter. I hope you can respond to my questions. I have enclosed a self-addressed stamped envelope should you choose to reply. I wish you all the best in your training and in your future races. I'll be cheering for you.

Sincerely,

Kelsey Walker

Respond to Reading

Read each question. Circle the letter next to your answer choice.

1. What does Kelsey hope to accomplish by writing the letter?

    a. describing the different segments of a triathlon

    b. requesting information from a triathlete

    c. explaining how to train for a triathlon

    d. showing the advantages of being a triathlete

2. Read the following excerpt.

> Swimming in the ocean for more than two miles, then biking 112 miles, finally running a 26-mile marathon must be exhausting, but you were able to complete the grueling course and set a personal best time.

Which word could replace *grueling* in the excerpt?

    f. remarkable

    g. enormous

    h. difficult

    j. fast

3. Kelsey organizes the information in the letter mostly by—

    a. providing anecdotes and then asking related questions.

    b. comparing the training routines of professionals and amateurs.

    c. describing problems triathletes have and then offering solutions.

    d. giving an opinion and reasons to convince the reader to run a race.

4. Which sentence from the letter best expresses the main idea?

    f. You inspire me, so I'm writing to learn more about you.

    g. My family has three triathletes—my brother, my mom, and me.

    h. Currently, I'm training for my first individual race, which will take place in August.

    j. I'm not concerned about the biking and running segments, but the swimming portion is another story.

Reread the letter on pages 63–64.

Think about what a reader learns from the author's personal stories. Organize your ideas. Use the chart below for prewriting.

Write a response in which you explain the effect of the author's use of first-person point of view. What is the reader able to understand from the author's personal stories? Use specific examples from the letter. Use your own sheet of paper.

Author's Personal Stories	What a Reader Learns

Be sure to—

1. explain the effect of the author's use of first-person point of view.

2. give evidence from the letter to support your ideas.

3. use linking words, such as *also, another,* and *but.*

4. use correct spelling, capitalization, punctuation, and grammar.

Formal Letter • *Genre Practice*

User Error

Read the passage below. Then answer the questions that follow.

I sat down at my desk one day
To surf the Internet.
I have a new computer here,
The best one you can get.

But when I pushed the power switch
It didn't even beep.
I tried again, but sure enough—
The CPU's asleep.

I stared a minute at the screen
Then sadly shook my head.
I pressed the button one more time
But my PC was dead.

It was working fine last night!
This does not compute!
I slowly faced the awful truth:
I'd need to troubleshoot.

I thought I'd better ask for help.
I yelled for brother John.
"You know a lot about these things,
So why won't it turn on?"

He looked it over once or twice
Then smiled at me and shrugged.
"You'd have some better luck," he said,
"If you had noticed it's unplugged."

Respond to Reading

Read each question. Circle the letter next to your answer choice.

1. "User Error" is an example of a narrative poem because it—

   a. is very short.

   b. includes rhyming words.

   c. tells a story.

   d. teaches a lesson.

2. How can you tell this poem is written in first-person point of view?

   f. The poet tells the poem directly to the reader.

   g. The poem is about something that happened to the poet.

   h. The poet speaks indirectly to the reader.

   j. The poet gives equal attention to both characters in the poem.

3. Read the third stanza in the poem. How does the poet likely feel?

   a. angry

   b. foolish

   c. encouraged

   d. frustrated

4. Read the last stanza of the poem. How do these lines relate to the poem's title?

   f. The poet is not tech-savvy and therefore needs help to fix the computer.

   g. The computer malfunction upsets the poet because the computer is new.

   h. The poet is embarrassed when John fixes the computer so easily.

   j. It was the poet's own mistake that caused the computer not to turn on.

Reread the poem "User Error" on page 67.

Think about the way the poet describes what is happening. How does this help you determine what the poet is feeling? Which clues does the poet give in each stanza to show how he or she feels? Organize your ideas. Use the space below for prewriting.

Write about the different feelings the poet of "User Error" experiences from the beginning of the poem to the end. Give evidence from the poem to support your ideas. Use your own sheet of paper.

Prewriting	
How does the poet feel in the first stanza?	How do you know?
How does the poet feel in the second stanza?	How do you know?
How does the poet feel in the third stanza?	How do you know?
How does the poet feel in the fourth stanza?	How do you know?
How does the poet feel in the fifth stanza?	How do you know?
How does the poet feel in the last stanza?	How do you know?

Be sure to—

1. describe what the poet is thinking and feeling in each stanza.

2. support your ideas with details from the poem that relate to the topic.

3. proofread, revise, and edit your writing as needed to improve clarity and eliminate mistakes.

Poetry • *Genre Practice*

Rock the Shades

Read the passage below. Then answer the questions that follow.

Characters

MR. HOLMES, music teacher
CASEY, a music student
ASCHA, CASEY'S friend and fellow student

(Music room. Mr. Holmes stands in front of a music stand stage left. Casey and Ascha sit in chairs stage right. They hold electric guitars plugged into amplifiers that sit to the side of each chair. Music stands are in front of them. Guitar cases are behind them. The curtain opens as Casey and Ascha finish playing the last two measures of a song.)

MR. HOLMES: *(After Casey and Ascha stop playing)* Good. OK, that'll do it for today. *(Casey and Ascha begin to pack up their sheet music.)* Oh, almost forgot. Speaking of good, I have some good news.

ASCHA: Oh, tell us!

MR. HOLMES: Well, this year the Spring Fair will end with a concert. Lots of local musicians will be performing, and that includes—you two!

CASEY: Wait. What?

ASCHA: Seriously?

MR. HOLMES: Yep, you star students will perform a duet at six o'clock. That's prime time! We'll have extra practices this week and next. *(Gathers sheet music on stand)* Don't be late. *(Turns and starts walking off stage left)* See you tomorrow.

(Ascha stands to grab her guitar case. Casey remains seated, looking at the floor.)

ASCHA: This is going to be so cool. Don't you think, Casey? *(Pause)* Casey? *(Puts down case and walks back to sit next to Casey)* Hey, what's wrong?

CASEY: *(Still looking at the floor)* Ascha . . . I . . . I . . . can't do the concert.

ASCHA: Why? You said you were going to the Spring Fair, so why can't you play at the Spring Fair?

CASEY: *(Looks up at Ascha)* It's just that . . . being on stage . . . that's not . . .

ASCHA: Oh, I get it. *(Casey looks back down at the floor.)* Look, it's perfectly normal to be nervous in front of an audience, and you won't be on the stage alone. I'll be there.

CASEY: I know, but . . .

ASCHA: Casey, you're an excellent guitar player, and people will be blown away by your skills.

CASEY: Yeah, but if I mess up . . .

ASCHA: OK, what's the worst thing that could happen if you mess up?

CASEY: I don't know. People will boo?

ASCHA: You really think people are going to boo two kids playing guitars at a Spring Fair? C'mon, even if you mess up, they'll still clap for us. Parents and teachers kind of do that.

CASEY: Yeah, OK, but what about the students?

ASCHA: We all get made fun of at some time or other, right? We'll just ignore them. Plus, we have lots of friends who can drown out any boos with more applause. Think of our friends as our own personal fan club.

CASEY: I guess, but . . .

ASCHA: But nothing. If the worst thing that can happen is that some kids boo us, well, that's not so bad. And by the way, when do YOU ever mess up? The chances of that happening are slim to none.

CASEY: I hear you, but playing in front of you and Mr. Holmes is different.

ASCHA: OK, brainstorm! Why don't we ask some people to sit in on our practices? That way you'll get used to performing in front of an audience.

CASEY: Yeah, that's a good idea. A better idea would be if I didn't have to see the audience at all.

ASCHA: OK, brainstorm part two. Sunglasses! Let's wear sunglasses. You can close your eyes, and no one will ever know.

CASEY: Sunglasses . . . (*Pause*) You know what? That just might work.

ASCHA: Uh-huh, we'll rock those sunglasses just like we'll rock the Spring Fair!

Play • *Genre Practice*

Name _____ Date _____

Respond to Reading

Read each questions. Circle the letter next to your answer choice.

1. What makes this selection a play?

    a. conflict   **c.** figurative language

    b. character tags   **d.** rhyme

2. Read the last two instances of dialogue between Casey and Ascha on page 71. The author uses stage directions to hint that Casey—

    f. knows he's been caught in a lie.

    g. thinks his guitar playing is bad.

    h. is anxious to leave the music room.

    j. is embarrassed about his stage fright.

3. Ascha helps Casey solve his problem by—

    a. offering him two ideas.

    b. making him feel guilty.

    c. performing by herself.

    d. requesting another partner.

4. Which of these is an important idea explored in the play?

    f. People who are loyal are rewarded.

    g. It takes courage to stand up for yourself.

    h. Friends help one another face challenges.

    J. Fear can make people lash out at others.

Reread "Rock the Shades" on pages 71–72.

Think about an adjective that describes Ascha and words from the play that support the description. What is Ascha's personality like? Organize your ideas. Use the graphic organizer below for prewriting. Write the adjective in the center circle. Write words from the play in the outer circles.

Write an essay explaining how the author's word choice contributes to Ascha's voice. Use specific examples from the play. Use your own sheet of paper.

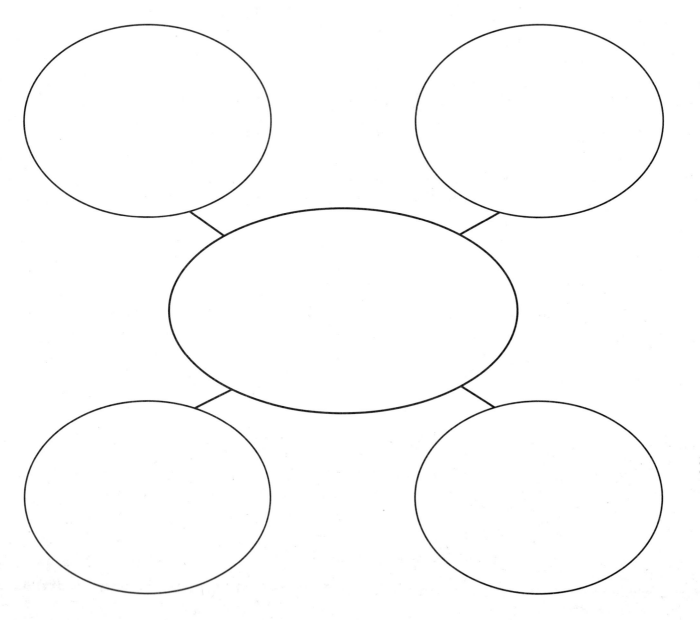

Be sure to—

1. explain how the author's word choice contributes to Ascha's voice.

2. provide specific examples from the play.

3. use linking words, such as *also, another,* and *but.*

4. use correct spelling, capitalization, punctuation, and grammar.

Play • *Genre Practice*

Davy Crockett and the Raccoon

**Read the passage below. Then answer the questions
that follow.**

Davy Crockett is an American hero known for his bravery, strength, and expert marksmanship. With his trusty rifle, Old Betsy, Davy was celebrated as an excellent hunter. Even the animals knew he was a good shot. And that is where this tale begins.

One day as Crockett and his faithful dog were walking home, a raccoon crossed their path. Upon seeing the raccoon, Davy's dog gave chase. The raccoon darted to the tallest tree and climbed up high in an effort to escape the dog's powerful jaws. The dog circled the tree, all the while barking and making sure the raccoon wouldn't escape until Crockett caught up.

When Crockett made it closer to the tree, he patted the dog's head and said, "All right now, you sit here, and let's see what we have." Crockett then walked to the base of the tree, looked up, and saw a raccoon with a back as wide as two ax handles and a ring-tail as long as the Rio Grande River. *Ah,* Crockett thought, *this varmint will provide good meat for my family and a good hide for a new hat.* Crockett swung Old Betsy from his shoulder and proceeded to take careful aim.

But before Crockett could take a shot, the raccoon turned to face him, revealing a face full of misery. The raccoon said to Crockett, "Are you the famous Davy Crockett, the brave and mighty hunter?"

Crockett was both surprised and flattered. Not only could this raccoon talk, but it also knew who Crockett was. And Crockett always enjoyed being recognized. He lowered Old Betsy and responded, "Why, yes, I am Davy Crockett."

"I thought so," said the raccoon, hanging its head. "Well," it added with a sigh, "I might as well come down this old tree then because I'm as good as dead. Everyone knows you never miss."

Crockett kept his rifle lowered and watched as the big raccoon made its way down the tree. Crockett couldn't help but feel a little sad for the critter. He thought, *This raccoon is so nice. Why, I can't harm it.*

When the raccoon finally made it to the ground, it turned to Crockett and waited. Crockett swung Old Betsy back onto his shoulder and said, "You are one special raccoon. I can't hurt you." He bent down and patted the raccoon on its head.

When Crockett straightened up, the raccoon cautiously began to back away toward the woods. All the while, it kept his eyes on Crockett and said, "That is mighty nice of you, Davy Crockett. You are as kind as you are fearless."

Crockett smiled, looked down, and shuffled his feet a bit. When he looked back up, the raccoon, still facing Davy, was standing at the edge of the woods. The raccoon stopped when it saw Crockett was once again looking at him.

"Now where you going?" asked Crockett, for he knew it wasn't every day a person got to talk with a raccoon, and he wanted to chat more.

"Home!" cried the raccoon. "Before you change your mind." Suddenly, the raccoon turned and ran as fast as a prairie fire with a tail wind into the forest, laughing all the way.

Crockett was smart enough to realize the big raccoon had played him like a fiddle, but what could he do? The raccoon had disappeared, so Crockett just laughed and laughed, but that was the last time a raccoon ever got the best of Davy Crockett.

Respond to Reading

Read each question. Circle the letter next to your answer choice.

1. This story contains—

    a. make-believe places.

    b. royal characters.

    c. larger-than-life events.

    d. repeated actions.

2. Read the following excerpt.

> Crockett was smart enough to realize the big raccoon had played him like a fiddle, but what could he do?

The author uses a simile to reveal Crockett—

    f. is confused about why the raccoon ran away.

    g. expects the raccoon to play an instrument.

    h. is unsure about how the raccoon could talk.

    j. understands the raccoon tricked him.

3. Why does the raccoon decide to climb down from the tree?

    a. It believes Crockett will be kind to him.

    b. It gives itself up because it knows Davy Crockett never misses a shot.

    c. It wants to show Crockett how brave it is.

    d. It thinks it will fall from the tree.

4. What lesson does Davy Crockett learn?

    f. Be cautious with those who praise too much.

    g. Boasting can lead to an embarrassing failure.

    h. Be polite to those who share a different view.

    j. Talking to animals can be dangerous.

Reread the third paragraph on page 75 and the fourth paragraph on page 76 of "Davy Crockett and the Raccoon."

Think about the ideas the hyperboles convey and how the exaggerated ideas affect readers. Organize your ideas. Use the chart below for prewriting.

Write an essay explaining how the author's use of exaggeration affects the story. Use specific examples from the story. What purpose do the hyperboles serve? Use your own sheet of paper.

Hyperbole	Idea Conveyed	Effect on Readers
Page 75:		
Page 76:		

Be sure to—

1. explain how the author's use of exaggeration affects the story.

2. use specific examples for the story.

3. connect ideas using linking words, such as *also, another,* and *but.*

4. use correct spelling, capitalization, punctuation, and grammar.

Beginnings in Japan

Read the passage below. Then answer the questions that follow.

Long ago, when the world was nothing more than mists and sea foam, the first generation of gods lived in the heavens. They knew the shapeless world needed to be made more substantial, so they assigned this task to the young gods Izanagi ("He Who Invites") and Izanami ("She Who Invites"). Izanagi and Izanami took the jeweled spear (called *Ama no Nuboko*) they were given and stood upon the Floating Bridge of Heaven, called *Ama-no-uki-hashi*. They looked down upon the mists and foam below.

They plunged Ama no Nuboko into the sea and stirred the murky water with its point. Then, as they lifted the spear up, drops of salty water falling from the tip formed the first piece of land, the first island. This was the Island of Onogoro.

Izanagi and Izanami descended the Floating Bridge of Heaven to live on the island, where they built a beautiful palace. In the very center of their palace they erected a pillar, called the Heavenly Pillar, which became Earth's axis.

Izanagi and Izanami decided to marry and begin a family. Izanagi said to Izanami, "Let us walk around the Heavenly Pillar. You circle it from the left, and I will go around from the right. When we meet, we will be wed."

The young gods walked around the pillar of the world in opposite directions.

When they met, Izanami spoke first, exclaiming with delight:

"What joy beyond compare
To see a man so fair!"

But Izanagi was angry with Izanami, because he felt he should have spoken first. He insisted they circle the Heavenly Pillar a second time to meet again. This time, Izanagi spoke first:

"To see a maid so fair—
What joy beyond compare!"

And so these were the first poems ever composed.

Soon after, Izanami gave birth to the Land of the Eight Great Islands of Japan, called *ho-ya-shima-kuni*. When the foam water solidified, many other smaller islands formed around it.

Then Izanagi again spoke to Izanami, saying, "We have now produced the Land of the Eight Great Islands, with all of its mountains, rivers, and trees. Let us now bring forth those who will look after our creation."

Together Izanagi and Izanami created the gods and goddesses of the sea, the wind, the trees, and the mountains and all other natural things.

And so the land of Japan was created.

Myth • *Genre Practice*

Name _____ Date _____

Respond to Reading

Read each question. Circle the letter next to your answer choice.

1. "Beginnings in Japan" is best characterized as a—

   a. myth, because it explains how something came to be.

   b. poem, because it includes rhyming words.

   c. legend, because it is based on "larger than life" characters.

   d. fable, because it teaches a lesson.

2. Izanagi and Izanami created the Island of Onogoro when they—

   f. descended the Floating Bridge of Heaven.

   g. circled the Heavenly Pillar.

   h. dipped a jeweled spear into the sea.

   j. composed the world's first poem.

3. Read this sentence from the story, and examine the italicized word.

   > They knew the *shapeless* world needed to be made more substantial, so they assigned this task to the young gods Izanagi ("He Who Invites") and Izanami ("She Who Invites").

   Based on the text, what is meaning of the suffix *-less*?

   a. resembling   c. containing

   b. without   d. able to be

4. What is the theme of this story?

   f. The gods are angered when humans misuse poetry and claim it as their own creation.

   g. It is impossible to fully enjoy life in the absence of beauty.

   h. The point of life is to pursue pleasure and avoid pain.

   j. Male and female energy create art as they cooperate and sometimes compete with each other.

Genre Practice • Myth

Lesson 20 **81**

Copyright © McGraw-Hill Education.

Reread the story "Beginnings in Japan" on pages 79–80.

Think about what the author is trying to achieve with this story. Why is a myth the best way to achieve this purpose? Organize your ideas. Use the space below for prewriting.

Write about how and why the author tells this story as a myth. Which characteristics of a myth are present in this selection? How does the author's choice of myth help express the theme? Give evidence from the story to support your ideas. Use your own paper or a paper provided by your teacher.

Prewriting	
Characteristics of a Myth	**Example from the Story**

Be sure to—

1. identify the characteristics of a myth that are present in the story.

2. explain why creating a myth is the best way for the author to tell this story.

3. support your ideas with details from the myth that relate to the topic.

4. proofread, revise, and edit your writing as needed to improve clarity and eliminate mistakes.

Myth • *Genre Practice*

What Plants Do in the Spring

Read both passages. Then answer the questions that follow.

Did you know green plants make their own food? Their stems and leaves contain tiny "food factories" that help them grow. Green plants need water, light, warmth, and nutrients to grow. And during spring, plants get the conditions they need to fire up their "food factories."

In spring, the hours of daylight get longer and longer. By the end of spring, most parts of the United States have between fourteen and sixteen hours of daylight each day. The weather in spring is often rainy, especially in April and May. This is good news for green plants!

The sun gives plants more light and warmth in the spring. The plants trap light energy from the sun in their leaves. A green pigment called chlorophyll absorbs light energy and stores it. During spring (and summer) the sun provides plenty of light, so plants make a lot of chlorophyll. Sunlight interacts with chlorophyll and other pigments to give plants their coloring. In spring, plants become green again because they are making so much chlorophyll.

Meanwhile, spring rains help the plants' roots take in water and nutrients from the soil. Tiny holes on the undersides of the leaves take in a gas called carbon dioxide.

The chlorophyll helps transform the stored light energy, the water, and the carbon dioxide into food for the plants. This food is a kind of sugar called glucose. The process of combining light energy, water, and carbon dioxide to make glucose is called photosynthesis. This is a compound word made from *photo-* (which means "light") and *synthesis* (which means "to put together").

The process of photosynthesis also releases oxygen into the atmosphere. This oxygen is what we breathe—we can't live without it. And some of the stored glucose plants produce during photosynthesis is stored in their fruits and roots. When we eat these foods, they give us energy too!

Spring Rolls In

It's the first day the air is warmer.
The sun beats down with stronger rays.
Dark clouds roll in and hide the sun.
A flash!
A crash!
It's springtime.

Winter's dryness and dull colors
are washed away,
as the old fallen leaves
make way for tiny new shoots.

The earth soaks up the rain.
The sun shines more each day.
It's the rain and the sun that
wake up the plants.
Then the leaves start to grow.

Some unfold,
others unravel.
Some of them pop,
while others whisper.

With their leaves spread out,
the plants can make food.
And with healthy plants growing all around,
that means there's more food for us!

Respond to Reading

Read each question. Circle the letter next to your answer choice.

1. Which element of informational text is present in the article "What Plants Do in the Spring"?

    a. It is meant to convince readers that a certain claim is true.

    b. It includes an emotional appeal to the reader.

    c. It attempts to persuade readers to act in a certain way.

    d. It describes a process in the order in which it happens.

2. Reread the second paragraph on page 83. Which sentence from the article is supported by this paragraph?

    f. The process of photosynthesis also releases oxygen into the atmosphere.

    g. During spring (and summer) the sun provides plenty of light, so plants make a lot of chlorophyll.

    h. Tiny holes on the undersides of the leaves take in a gas called carbon dioxide.

    j. Green plants need water, light, warmth, and nutrients to grow.

3. What kind of writing is "Spring Rolls In"?

    a. It is explanatory text because tells how something works.

    b. It is a poem because it contains lines, verses, and stanzas.

    c. It is a narrative because it has a beginning, middle, and end.

    d. It is rhyming nonfiction because it presents factual information.

4. Read the following lines from "Spring Rolls In."

    > Some of them pop,
    > while others whisper.

    Which literary device is found in these lines?

    f. alliteration   **h.** simile

    g. hyperbole   **j.** onomatopoeia

5. What is one way the two selections are similar?

 a. They discuss similar topics.

 b. They are intended to inform the reader.

 c. They are organized in chronological order.

 d. They contain facts that can be checked in another source.

6. What is one difference between the two selections?

 f. One is meant to be read, and the other is meant to be performed in front of an audience.

 g. One uses exaggeration to explain how something came to be, and the other uses rhymes.

 h. One is meant to explain, and the other is intended to persuade.

 j. One provides factual information, and the other is written figuratively.

7. Which idea is in both selections?

 a. People need the oxygen created by plants.

 b. Spring is a time of new plant growth.

 c. Chlorophyll absorbs light energy and stores it.

 d. Spring is most people's favorite time of year.

8. Which idea is in only one of the selections?

 f. Plants use sunlight and water to make food.

 g. Plants begin to grow rapidly in April and May.

 h. Plants provide energy to the people who eat them.

 j. Plants become green in spring.

Comparing Genres • *Genre Practice*

Comparing Genres

Reread the selections "What Plants Do in the Spring" and "Spring Rolls In" on pages 83–84.

Think about each author's purpose. What do the authors want you to think about spring? What is their purpose? In your opinion, do the authors achieve that purpose successfully? Do they seem to feel the same way toward spring? How do you know? Organize your ideas. Use the space below for prewriting.

Write about how successfully the authors of each selection talk about similar ideas in different ways. Why do they do this? Give evidence from the story to support your ideas. Use your own paper or a paper provided by your teacher.

Prewriting		
	"What Plants Do in the Spring"	"Spring Rolls In"
What kind of passage is this? How do you know?		
Why did the author write this passage?		
What kinds of words does the author use to describe the process of photosynthesis?		
What does the author want you to think when you finish reading? How do the author's words help you feel this way?		

Be sure to—

1. describe how the authors of each selection use different styles to talk about similar ideas.

2. explain why each author uses this kind of language.

3. state an opinion about how successfully the authors achieve their purpose.

4. support your opinion with details from the selections that relate to the topic.

Revising

Use this checklist to revise your opinion writing.

- Does your writing have a clear purpose?
- Does your writing state an opinion?
- Does your writing have reasons that support your opinion?
- Does your writing include interesting details or descriptions?
- Did you include an ending that sums up your opinion?

Editing/Proofreading

Use this checklist to correct mistakes in your opinion writing.

- Did you use proofreading symbols when editing?
- Does your writing include transition words?
- Did you check for subject/verb agreement?
- Did you check your writing for spelling mistakes?

Publishing

Use this checklist to prepare your opinion writing for publishing.

- Write or type a neat copy of your writing.
- Add a photograph or a drawing if it enhances your writing.

Comparing Genres • *Genre Practice*

Gregor Mendel and Heredity

Read the passage below. Then answer the questions that follow.

Do you ever wonder why two sisters look almost like twins or why one of two brothers is extremely tall but the other is of average height or why parents who have blond hair have a child with red hair? You're not the only one who has thought about why people look the way they do. More than one hundred fifty years ago, in 1856, Gregor Mendel pondered similar questions.

The Scientist

Gregor Mendel was an Austrian monk and a botanist, a scientist who studies plants. In addition to plants, Mendel also had a keen interest in heredity, or the passing of traits from one generation to the next. By combining his knowledge of plants with his interest in heredity, Mendel set out to better understand how traits pass from generation to generation. After eight years of careful and systematic research, he made some important discoveries.

The Discovery

Mendel's research led him to discover the principles of inherited traits. How did Mendel go about making these discoveries? He did so by experimenting with pea plants in the garden of his monastery. First, Mendel crossed two different types of pea plants: Plant A had smooth peas; plant B had wrinkled peas. These two parent plants created offspring plants that produced only smooth peas. Next, Mendel crossed the offspring plants. They in turn created plants that produced both smooth and wrinkled peas. Wrinkled peas had returned in this second generation!

Mendel also conducted an experiment with pea plants that had pods of different colors; one plant had green pods and one had yellow pods. These parent plants produced children plants with only yellow pods. The children plants with yellow pods produced plants with both yellow and green pods. Similar to the wrinkled peas, green pods had returned in the second generation.

Mendel, though, didn't stop with two experiments. In total, he tested seven traits of pea plants—seed form, pod color, seed color, flower color, pod shape, flower location, and plant height. From these experiments, Mendel concluded three principles:

- Traits are passed from one generation to another.
- Each trait is made of two units, one for each parent.
- Some traits are dominant and appear more often, such as round and yellow, while other traits are recessive and may skip generations, like wrinkled and green.

From Peas to People

Even though Mendel published his discoveries in 1866, his work wasn't recognized until after his death. Nearly forty years after Mendel published his results, scientists studying heredity came across his research and found that the results from their experiments were similar to Mendel's. This encouraged scientists to research heredity even more—in plants, in animals, and in humans. The new science of genetics emerged and grew.

Because Mendel's discoveries are the principles by which scientists study heredity today, Mendel is now considered the Father of Genetics.

Writing to Sources • *Genre Practice*

Respond to Reading

Read each question, then write your answers on the lines. For questions that ask you to underline text evidence, mark your answers on pages 89–90.

1. According to the selection, why did Mendel conduct experiments on pea plants?

_____

_____

_____

_____

2. According to the selection, which traits did Mendel study when he conducted experiments on pea plants? <u>Underline</u> the text where it provides this information.

_____

_____

_____

_____

3. According to the selection, what principles did Mendel's experiments reveal? Paraphrase the three principles.

_____

_____

_____

_____

4. What does *genetics* mean?

_____

_____

_____

_____

5. Draw a diagram that represents Mendel's experiment with smooth and wrinkled pea plants described on page 89. Draw the parent Plant A and parent Plant B, their offspring plants, and the third-generation plants. Add lines between parents and offspring plants.

6. Write an explanation of how the author's use of headings helps you understand the selection. Which headings do you find helpful and why? Which headings would you change and why?

_____

_____

_____

_____

_____

_____

_____

_____

_____

Writing to Sources • *Genre Practice*

Pecos Bill and the Tornado

Read the passage below. Then answer the questions that follow.

I suppose just about everybody has heard of Pecos Bill by now. He was the greatest cowboy Texas has ever seen. Why, all the other cowboys used a regular old lasso to rope cattle, but that was too easy for Bill. He liked to use the biggest, meanest rattlesnake he could find to rope cattle. He'd work up such an appetite, only a plateful of dynamite for supper could satisfy him. And he was a crack shot with his pistol too. One night he shot every star clean out of the sky just to impress his girlfriend, Slue-Foot Sue. He did leave one star shining, though—and that one became the Texas Lone Star.

Now Bill loved riding horses, and he could ride anything. No bronco was so wild that Bill couldn't tame it after just a minute or two. After riding every bronco and bull in the state of Texas, Bill decided he needed something more challenging to ride. So he declared he was going to ride a tornado. But not just a puny, pint-sized tornado. No ma'am! Bill waited it out until the biggest, curliest, twirliest tornado the clouds ever produced came whamming out of the sky. Why, that tornado was so big, the folks far away in New York City heard it coming and took cover! But Bill wasn't afraid one bit. He reached up with one hand and grabbed that tornado right out of the sky. Then he tossed it to the ground just as easy as pie and jumped right on.

Don't you know that tornado heaved and rocked and bucked like a dragon with a thorn in its tail? But Bill held on just as cool as a cucumber and jabbed it with his spurs to calm it down. And didn't that make that old tornado angry! It spun around and headed straight through the big forests in Kansas and flattened every one of those trees, so they had to rename that place the Great Plains. Then the tornado headed west and plowed right through part of the Rocky Mountains out there. It twisted and twirled and leaped and dropped, trying to throw ol' Bill off. Its powerful trailing tail dragged across the ground and carved out a Grand Canyon that folks like to visit even today! But no matter what tricks it tried, Bill wouldn't let go.

Finally, the tornado plum wore itself out and stopped its whirling and twirling, and Bill fell off. He fell so hard the ground sank below sea level. Folks named that spot Death Valley. But Bill just laughed, brushed the dust off his jacket, let out a big holler, and headed on back to Texas.

Bill's tornado ride became famous, and that's where the other cowboys got the idea for rodeos. But these days most cowboys stay away from tornadoes.

Tall Tale • *Genre Practice*

Respond to Reading

Read each question. Circle the letter next to your answer choice.

1. Which detail from the story is characteristic of a tall tale?

    a. Cowboys use lassos to rope cattle.

    b. Pecos Bill rides a tornado and jabs it with his spurs.

    c. Death Valley is a place that is below sea level.

    d. Pecos Bill is extremely skilled at riding wild horses.

2. What real-life event probably influenced the plot of this story?

    f. Tornado damage created the Great Plains.

    g. The King of Siam was familiar with Pecos Bill.

    h. Cowboys in Texas likely experienced actual tornadoes.

    j. Cowboys commonly used rattlesnakes as lassos.

3. Why does Pecos Bill decide to ride a tornado?

    a. He wants to help create the Grand Canyon.

    b. He was bored with riding broncos.

    c. He wanted to show how tough he was.

    d. He wanted to impress Slue-Foot Sue.

4. Which idea does "Pecos Bill and the Tornado" BEST express?

    f. Many cowboys of the Old West took foolish chances and lived precarious lives.

    g. Western pioneers of the nineteenth century faced great dangers and hardships.

    h. American expansion into the West was both justified and inevitable.

    j. Early settlers of the American West believed there were no limits to what they could do.

Reread the story "Pecos Bill and the Tornado" on pages 93–94.

Think about why someone might be interested in tall tales about Pecos Bill. What do hyperbole, humor, and figurative language add to this story? Who is telling the story? What is the storyteller's attitude toward Pecos Bill? Why might someone admire such a hero? What has the author done to make readers like Pecos Bill and his adventures? Organize your ideas. Use the space below for prewriting.

Write about why tall tales about characters like Pecos Bill are popular. Give evidence from the story to support your ideas. Use your own paper or a paper provided by your teacher.

Prewriting	
Characteristics of a Tall Tale	**Examples from the Story**
Hyperbole	
Humorous Tone	
Voice/Everyday Language	
Figurative Language/Similes	

Be sure to—

1. describe the characteristics of a tall tale that are present in the story.

2. explain why the author uses hyperbole, humor, and simile to tell this story.

3. examine why people enjoy reading stories about Pecos Bill.

4. support your ideas with details from the story that relate to the topic.

5. proofread, revise, and edit your writing as needed to improve clarity and eliminate mistakes.

Tall Tale • *Genre Practice*

Students and Freedom of Expression

Read the passage below. Then answer the questions that follow.

Congress shall make no law . . . prohibiting the free exercise thereof; or abridging the freedom of speech . . .

First Amendment, Bill of Rights

The First Amendment of the Bill of Rights guarantees the freedom of expression. Americans have the right to share ideas and opinions without being afraid they will be punished. The right extends to all Americans, both old and young. Does that mean students in school can say what they want? Can they express themselves freely without being punished?

Some may argue that the answers to these questions should always be yes. When students enter a school, they do not leave their First Amendment rights outside. Therefore, students should be able to share opinions—even opinions others may disagree with—inside their school. For example, if students dislike a school rule that bans cell phones, they should be allowed to say so. By being permitted to voice their concerns, students not only experience freedom of expression, but they also learn to value that freedom.

Others, though, would say that giving students unlimited free speech could lead to problems within the school. If students are allowed to say whatever they want, some may decide to make hurtful remarks to their classmates or to say things that disrupt their classes. Is the right of one student to speak freely more important than the rights of other students to feel accepted and to learn? The answer to this question would be no.

In 1969, the Supreme Court ruled on student speech. In the case of *Tinker vs. Des Moines,* the Supreme Court confirmed the First Amendment right of students—but with limits. The court said students have the right to speak their minds in school, and school administrators cannot punish students for asserting that right, as long as the students' speech does not cause a disruption.

Having boundaries about what can and cannot be said in a school is one way to teach students about how free speech works. While the First Amendment guarantees free speech as a right, it does not define what free speech is. The people do that by electing officials to write laws about what is appropriate to say and not say.

Laws that limit speech are part of the world beyond school too. For example, in the adult world, a person cannot threaten another without consequences. A person cannot spread false claims about another in public without consequences. A person cannot use language to start a fight without consequences. These limits of free speech in public and in schools are there for a reason: to protect others.

Because schools are designed to prepare students to live as adults, schools should set boundaries of free speech just as there are boundaries within the adult world. However, limited speech doesn't mean students are prevented from speaking. On the contrary, students should be taught how to express their opinions appropriately, without causing disruptions or attacking others. They should be taught how to share their opinions, provide reasons for holding those opinions, and support their opinions with facts and evidence. Students should be taught how to listen to others, especially to those with different viewpoints. For example, those students who disagree with a cell phone ban could write an article for their school newspaper, circulate a petition, or present their argument to school officials. Free speech is a right students should exercise, but they should do so in a way that is not harmful to others.

Argumentative Text • *Genre Practice*

Respond to Reading

Read each question. Circle the letter next to your answer choice.

1. The main purpose of this selection is to—

   a. reason that students' freedom of expression should be limited.

   b. compare students' freedom of expression to adults'.

   c. explain why being able to speak freely is important.

   d. describe different ways people express themselves.

2. Read the following excerpt.

   > The court said students have the right to speak their minds in school, and school administrators cannot punish students for asserting that right, as long as the students' speech does not cause a disruption.

   The word *asserting* could be replaced with which word?

   f. debating   **h.** claiming

   g. surrendering   **j.** blocking

3. Which sentence from the selection is an opinion?

   a. The First Amendment of the Bill of Rights guarantees the freedom of expression.

   b. In 1969, the Supreme Court ruled on student speech.

   c. A person cannot use language to start a fight without consequences.

   d. They should be taught how to listen to others, especially to those with different viewpoints.

4. Which statement best expresses the author's main idea?

   f. Because freedom of expression does not have an age limit, students should be able to express themselves in any way they choose.

   g. While free speech is a right to all people, students' free speech should be limited in order to protect the rights of other students.

   h. Students should be allowed to say whatever they want and not be punished, just like adults.

   j. Students are allowed to share opinions, but only when they leave school.

Reread "Students and Freedom of Expression" on pages 97–98.

Think about what the author thinks and the evidence the author provides to convince readers to agree with him or her. What evidence does the author provide? How does the author address readers who may disagree with the author's opinion? Organize your ideas. Use the graphic organizer below for prewriting.

Write an explanation of the author's support for his or her claim. Use specific examples from the selection. Use your own sheet of paper.

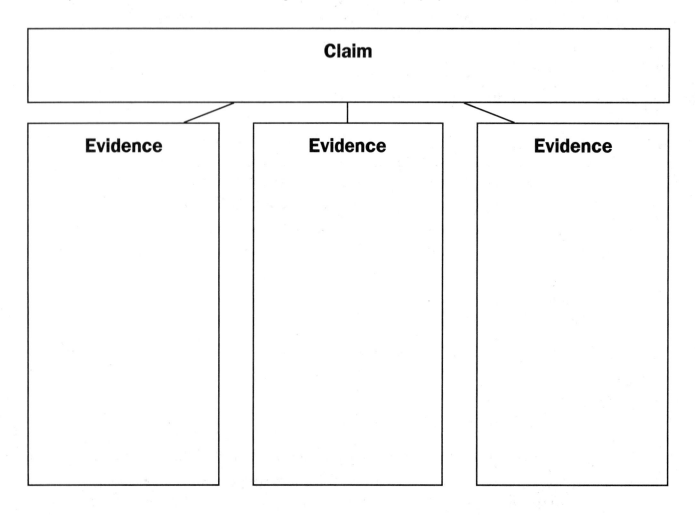

Be sure to—

1. explain how the author supports his or her claim.

2. support your ideas with evidence from the selection.

3. use linking words, such as *also, another,* and *but.*

4. use correct spelling, capitalization, punctuation, and grammar.

Argumentative Text • *Genre Practice*

Rip Van Winkle

Read the passage below. Then answer the questions that follow.

In a pretty village at the foot of the Catskill Mountains lived a kind man named Rip Van Winkle. Rip was beloved by his neighbors, especially the children, as he always had stories to share. No one had anything unpleasant to say about Rip except his wife, who nagged him mercilessly.

One day, Rip fled from his wife's scolding by going hunting in the woods with his dog Wolf. When evening approached, they slowly began making their way home. It was then that Rip encountered an odd little man with a beard and wild hair. The man was dressed in old-fashioned clothes, like the kind one might see in old Dutch paintings. He carried a large container and motioned for help. Rip, always generous, took the container and assisted the little man up the mountain.

As they walked, rumblings like thunder could be heard in the valley below. Upon entering the valley, Rip was greeted with an extraordinary sight. Several little men, similar to his companion, were playing ninepins. Each time they rolled the ball toward the pins, Rip heard the rumbling noise.

Rip lowered the container onto the ground. His companion opened it and motioned for Rip to pour liquid from it into the other men's cups. Rip, curious about the liquid, took a sip as well. The liquid made him sleepy, so he lay on the ground and fell into a deep sleep.

In the morning, Rip found himself not in the valley but in the same place where he met the little man. At first, Rip thought the men were part of a strange dream, but upon seeing that his new rifle had been replaced with a rusty one, he knew they weren't. "They stole my rifle," Rip exclaimed, "and where is Wolf?"

With difficulty, because his joints were stiff, Rip returned to the village. To his amazement, the village had grown overnight. Where once were meadows were now houses. As he wandered about trying to locate a familiar place, people began to gather around him. They asked who he was. Rip was startled. "Does anyone here know Rip Van Winkle?" he asked.

"Yes," one man said, "he's there, leaning against the tree." Rip gazed at the man, who looked very similar to him. Rip was confused.

At that time, a woman named Judith Gardenir approached the group. She looked familiar, so Rip asked her who her father was. She answered, "My poor father was Rip Van Winkle. He left twenty years ago to go hunting, and while his dog returned home, he never did."

Rip then asked Judith where her mother was. "She died too."

It was then that Rip cried out, "I'm your father! Don't you recognize me?"

Everyone looked at Rip in disbelief until Peter Vanderdonk, the oldest man in the village, stepped forward and peered closely at him. "Why, yes, this is Rip Van Winkle!"

Suddenly, everyone wanted to know what had happened to him, so Rip relayed his story. "Ah," said Peter, "you met the spirits of Hendrick Hudson, the discoverer of this region, and his men. They return to the area to keep watch over the river. My father once saw them playing ninepins in the valley, making thunderous noise." And with that, the group left Rip to reunite with his children.

Soon Rip returned to his old life, telling stories to the village children and to any traveler who happened to be visiting. Some people didn't believe Rip's tale, but others did, and whenever they heard a thunderstorm, they would say Hendrick Hudson was playing ninepins with his crew.

Folktale • *Genre Practice*

Respond to Reading

Read each question. Circle the letter next to your answer choice.

1. What event from the story is commonly found in folktales?

   a. a main character travels

   b. a story is told over and over

   c. a search for a special object takes place

   d. a character vanishes mysteriously

2. Reread the first three paragraphs on page 102. Rip's hesitation to reveal his identity shows that Rip—

   f. was not convinced Judith was his daughter.

   g. was not able to remember who he was.

   h. did not want to see his wife.

   j. did not want to upset his daughter.

3. How does the setting impact the story?

   a. The mountains symbolize hope.

   b. The woods present problems the main character must solve.

   c. The evening hours create a joyful mood.

   d. The change in the village's size shows time passed.

4. Which sentence best summarizes the selection?

   f. Rip Van Winkle hides from his nagging wife by going hunting in the woods.

   g. Rip Van Winkle drinks a mysterious liquid, falls asleep, and wakes years later.

   h. Rip Van Winkle discovers strange little men who live in the Catskill Mountains.

   j. Rip Van Winkle returns to his village and searches for friends, but no one recognizes him.

Reread the third paragraph on page 101 and the fifth paragraph on 102 of "Rip Van Winkle."

Think about what the paragraphs explain and how this explanation relates to folktales. Organize your ideas. Use the chart below for prewriting.

Write an essay that explains the purpose of these paragraphs. Why does the author include them? Use evidence from the selection. Use your own sheet of paper.

Story Detail	What the Detail Explains	How the Explanation Relates to Folktales

Be sure to—

1. explain the purpose of the two paragraphs.

2. support your ideas with evidence from the story.

3. use linking words, such as *also, another,* and *but.*

4. use correct spelling, capitalization, punctuation, and grammar.

Folktale • *Genre Practice*

Is This Vegetarian?

Read the passage below. Then answer the questions that follow.

Imagine a plate full of rainbow-colored food—a bed of green leafy spinach topped with slices of red bell pepper, orange carrots, small yellow tomatoes, green snap peas, blueberries, and slivers of golden toasted almonds. To the right of this plate is another piled with warm toasted bread. Notice anything missing? If you said meat, you're correct. This colorful meal is being served to a vegetarian.

For different reasons, many people are turning to vegetarian, or meat-free, diets. Some choose to avoid meat for ethical reasons, believing that animals should not be raised for food. Others decide to become vegetarians for health reasons. Vegetarian diets are often lower in saturated fat and cholesterol, so they can help reduce the risk of heart disease. Whatever the reason, plant-based diets are common today.

Being a vegetarian, though, takes skill. Why? Because the food we eat, especially packaged food, is not always what it appears to be. Some foods you might think of as vegetarian are really not, because they are made with animal ingredients. For example, a box of Spanish rice may not be vegetarian if it is made with chicken fat. Flour tortillas are often made with lard, or pig fat, and Caesar salad dressing may contain anchovies, tiny fish that add a salty flavoring to food. To avoid foods made with animal products, vegetarians must learn how to read labels.

Reading food labels, though, can be tricky. Sure, some of the ingredients are familiar, but some look like words straight from a chemistry textbook. However, with a little practice and patience, vegetarians can learn which ingredients to avoid, even if they aren't obviously described as animal products.

Let's review a label we might find on a can of vegetable soup. The first thing to look at is cholesterol, which is found under nutrition facts. If a product has any cholesterol, it contains an animal ingredient. The cholesterol for the vegetable soup is 0 grams, but that doesn't mean it is vegetarian. We need to continue checking other areas of the label. The second place to look for animal products is under the allergy listings. The allergy list will let vegetarians who want to avoid dairy know if a product contains milk or milk products. Note that the allergy list on the can of soup lists only wheat as an allergen. So far, this soup is appropriate for a vegetarian.

We still need to check one last place, and that's the ingredient list. Read the ingredient list carefully, noting any obvious meat ingredients and any not-so-obvious ones. To recognize the less obvious animal-based products, especially those with scientific names, you'll need to commit them to memory, print a list and carry it with you, or use an app. A review of the soup's ingredients reveals two problems for a vegetarian the other areas on the label did not. The soup is made with beef stock, an obvious meat product, and modified food starch, a less obvious source of animal-based products that is sometimes made with animal fat. The inclusion of both of these ingredients means this soup is not appropriate for a vegetarian.

Reading labels may seem both difficult and time consuming, but many vegetarians find that, over time, practice makes perfect. They become so familiar with different ingredients that they are able to scan a food's label quickly to determine if it is suitable to eat. And for vegetarians, taking this extra step of recognizing the ingredients in a packaged item helps them stay committed to their plant-based diet.

Canned Vegetable Soup Food Label

NUTRITION FACTS

Serving Size ½ cup

Amount/Serving	
Calories	80
Calories from Fat	15
Total Fat	1.5g
Saturated Fat	0g
Trans Fat	0g
Cholesterol	0g
Sodium	890mg
Potassium	170mg
Carbohydrate Total	14g
Fiber	2g
Sugars	2g
Protein	2g

INGREDIENTS:
Beef Stock, Carrots, Potatoes, Celery, Enriched Pasta (Enriched Wheat Flour [Wheat, Niacin, Ferrous Sulfate, Thiamine Mononitrate, Riboflavin, Folic Acid]), Peas, Corn, Green Beans, Tomato Puree (Water, Tomato Paste), Cabbage, **Modified Food Starch,** Contains Less Than 2% Of: Salt, Onions, Vegetable Oil, Yeast Extract, Celery Leaves, Monosodium Glutamate, Dehydrated Onions, Hydrolyzed Soy Protein, Caramel Color, Parsley, Hydrolyzed Wheat Gluten.

CONTAINS WHEAT

Informational Text • *Genre Practice*

Respond to Reading

Read each question. Circle the letter next to your answer choice.

1. The author informs readers about the challenges that face vegetarians mainly by—
   a. describing the reasons people choose to become vegetarians.
   b. explaining how vegetarians must read labels thoroughly.
   c. listing foods that vegetarians should not eat.
   d. presenting the benefits of a vegetarian diet.

2. Which statement from the selection best explains why food labels are important to vegetarians?
   f. Vegetarian diets are often lower in saturated fat and cholesterol, so they can help reduce the risk of heart disease.
   g. Because the food we eat, especially packaged food, is not always what it appears to be.
   h. Sure, some of the ingredients are familiar, but some look like words straight from a chemistry textbook.
   j. Reading labels may seem both difficult and time consuming, but many vegetarians find that, over time, practice makes perfect.

3. What is the most likely reason the author includes the image of a food label with the selection?
   a. to show where information about animal products can be found
   b. to show the amount of information a food label can provide
   c. to show the nutritional value of vegetable soup
   d. to show the number of ingredients in vegetable soup

4. Which sentence best summarizes the selection?
   f. Packaged foods that seem vegetarian may contain meat products.
   g. People who choose not to eat meat do so for a number of reasons.
   h. Food labels provide information about nutrition, allergens, and ingredients.
   j. Reading food labels can help vegetarians select packaged foods that are truly plant based.

Reread the first two paragraphs on page 106.

Think about how the details in these paragraphs are organized. Look for signal words. What does this type of organization help readers understand? Organize your ideas. Use the graphic organizer below for prewriting.

Write an essay explaining how the organizational structure of the fifth and sixth paragraphs in the selection contributes to the author's purpose. Use specific evidence from the selection. Use your own sheet of paper.

Signal Words

```
┌─────────────────────────────────────────────────┐
│                                                   │
│                                                   │
│                                                   │
│                                                   │
└─────────────────────────────────────────────────┘
                          │
                          ▼
```

Organizational Structure

```
┌─────────────────────────────────────────────────┐
│                                                   │
│                                                   │
│                                                   │
│                                                   │
└─────────────────────────────────────────────────┘
                          │
                          ▼
```

Author's Purpose

```
┌─────────────────────────────────────────────────┐
│                                                   │
│                                                   │
│                                                   │
│                                                   │
└─────────────────────────────────────────────────┘
```

Be sure to—

1. explain how the organization of the fifth and sixth paragraphs contributes to the author's purpose.

2. support your ideas with evidence from the selection.

3. use linking words, such as *also, another,* and *but.*

4. use correct spelling, capitalization, punctuation, and grammar.

Informational Text • *Genre Practice*

Name _____ Date _____

Pecos Bill and Slue-Foot Sue

Read the passage below. Then answer the questions that follow.

Now there's never been a greater cowboy than Pecos Bill. In fact, he invented the art of being a cowboy. When he came across a cow that wouldn't behave, he'd just jump on its back and ride until it plumb tuckered out and started behaving better. But the other cowboys weren't as skillful as Bill, so he came up with the idea of throwing a lariat over a cow's head to tame 'em. Of course, being Pecos Bill he used a rattlesnake for a lariat instead of a rope.

Now Bill had a horse named Widowmaker. And Widowmaker was the strongest, fastest horse that ever lived. Bill and Widowmaker traveled all over creation, and no one could ride that horse but Bill. The truth is, no one ever dared to try. And that's how it should have been.

But one day, Bill and Widowmaker were moseying down by the Pecos River when they spied a woman—and not just any woman. No sir! She had great big green eyes and wild red hair, and she was whooping and hollering almost as loud as Bill did when he rode old Widowmaker. And don't you know this woman was riding on the back of a catfish nearly as big as a whale, right down the middle of the Pecos? And Bill fell in love with her, right there on the spot.

Her name was Slue-Foot Sue. She lived on a ranch with her mother and father, and she enjoyed cowboying almost as much as Bill did. Well, Bill wouldn't rest until he asked for her hand in marriage. And Slue-Foot Sue agreed.

On their wedding day, Bill wore his best buckskin suit, and Sue wore a beautiful white dress with a big steel-spring bustle in the back. It was the kind of hooped skirt that women wore back in those days—the bigger the better! But for some reason, right after the wedding Sue got it in her head to have a ride on old Widowmaker. Bill tried to talk her out of it, of course, but Sue was dying to have a ride on that horse. She figured if Bill could ride Widowmaker, she could too.

You might guess what happened. The second Sue jumped on Widowmaker's back he began to kick and buck. Sue couldn't hold on for long, and quicker than a cat can lick its eye, Widowmaker sent her flying into the Texas sky. Sue went higher than the hills, higher than the mesas, even higher than the mountains. Why, she flew so high that she sailed clean over the moon! Sue was still wearing her springy hoop, of course, so when she fell back down and hit the ground, she just bounced right back up again.

Now this went on for days, and Bill figured Sue would keep bouncing forever if he didn't try to stop her. So he lassoed her with his rattlesnake lariat to catch her and bring her back down to Earth. But don't you know she just yanked him back up with her! And they never came back down.

Folks figure that Bill and Sue must've landed on the moon and decided to stay there. They must've raised a family, too, because the thunder that carries over the Pecos River is much louder and wilder now than it was before. And that could only be Pecos Bill's family just laughing up a storm.

Tall Tale • *Genre Practice*

Respond to Reading

Read each question. Circle the letter next to your answer choice.

1. What is one way you can identify this story as a tall tale?

    a. its use of exaggeration

    b. its use of real facts

    c. its sad ending

    d. its use of romance

2. Based on the author's word choice, what is the setting of "Pecos Bill and Slue-Foot Sue"?

    f. colonial New England

    g. 19th-century western frontier

    h. Pacific Northwest

    j. modern-day Texas

3. Which quote from the story foreshadows the main action of the plot?

    a. Now there's never been a greater cowboy than Pecos Bill. In fact, he invented the art of being a cowboy.

    b. Bill and Widowmaker traveled all over creation, and no one could ride that horse but Bill. The truth is, no one ever dared to try. And that's how it should have been.

    c. Being Pecos Bill he used a rattlesnake for a lariat instead of a rope.

    d. They must've raised a family, too, because the thunder that carries over the Pecos River is much louder and wilder now that it was before.

4. What is the best summary of "Pecos Bill and Slue-Foot Sue"?

    f. Slue-Foot Sue fails to ride the wild bronco, Widowmaker, proving that Pecos Bill is indeed the greatest cowboy in all of Texas.

    g. Pecos Bill tries to warn his wife, Slue-Foot Sue, that no one has ever been able to ride his horse, Widowmaker. Sue is embarrassed when she is thrown from the horse after one try.

    h. When Slue-Foot Sue tries to ride Widowmaker, she is thrown off and bounces between the moon and Earth until Pecos Bill lassos her. They are both carried to the moon, where they settle and raise a family.

    j. Pecos Bill meets his match when he spies a woman named Slue-Foot Sue riding a giant catfish down the middle of the Pecos River. They fall in love and have several children.

Reread "Pecos Bill and Slue-Foot Sue" on pages 109–110.

Think about why the author wrote "Pecos Bill and Slue-Foot Sue." How does the ending make you feel? Do you think this is a good ending? Would another ending have been better? In some versions, after Pecos Bill lassos Slue-Foot Sue, she decides the cowboy life is not for her, and Pecos Bill sadly rides away without her. What kind of ending do you think is most appropriate? Organize your ideas. Use the space below for prewriting.

Write about the ending of this story. Explain your ideas with details from the story. Use your own paper or paper provided by your teacher.

What Is the Author's Purpose?	How Does the Story End?	How Does the Ending Affect the Story?	How Would a Different Ending Change the Story?

Copyright © McGraw-Hill Education.

Be sure to—

1. describe the ending of the story.

2. tell how the ending makes you feel and whether you think it is a good ending.

3. explain whether you think another ending would (or would not) be better.

4. support your opinions with details from the story.

5. proofread, revise, and edit your writing as needed to improve clarity and eliminate mistakes.

Tall Tale • *Genre Practice*

Name _____ Date _____

The Yellow Emperor

Read the passage below. Then answer the questions that follow

It is said that all Chinese people have a common ancestor: Huangdi, or the "Yellow Emperor." He was the first ruler of the land that would later become China. His reign began in 2697 B.C.E. when he united the tribes of the Yellow River plain under a single government.

The Yellow Emperor lived in a fabulous palace in the Kunlun Mountains, guarded by a human-headed tiger with nine tails. The emperor was able to speak just moments after his birth and was said to have four faces that could gaze upon his lands in four different directions. Whenever he traveled, he rode in a chariot made of ivory and pulled by dragons and an elephant. The Yellow Emperor loved the rare creatures that lived in the mountains, and was accompanied wherever he went by a procession of animals.

The Yellow Emperor brought civilization to China, and he gave the people many useful items. He himself taught the people how to hunt and how to build houses so they would no longer need to live in caves and trees. When he saw people walking wearily, he invented wheeled vehicles for them to ride in. He gave them the calendar so they would know when to sow and harvest their fields, and gave them the compass so they would never be lost. And his dialogues with his physician, Qi Bo, formed the basis of China's first medical book, the *Huangdi Neijing (or The Yellow Emperor's Classic of Medicine)*.

The emperor's wife, Lei Zu, taught Chinese women how to breed silkworms and spin their silk into exquisite clothing. Huangdi also commanded his ministers Li Shou to invent mathematics and Cang Jie to invent China's alphabet. For all these gifts, the Chinese still revere the Yellow Emperor as a wise and generous ruler.

One of the emperor's greatest gifts was music. Once, his rival Chi You challenged him to battle. Chi You used magic to cover the battlefield in fog, bewildering the Yellow Emperor and his army. Then the fairy Xuan Nu appeared to him in a dream, instructing the emperor to produce battle drums made with the skin of the Kui—a fiendish monster that lived on the shores of the Eastern Sea. The thunderous charge of the battle drums boosted his army's morale and sent Chi You's forces scattering. As the story goes, his own troops were also shaken by the thunderous sound of the drums, so he invented a plucked-string instrument whose tranquil music could sooth their spirits.

After ruling for 100 years, the Yellow Emperor abdicated the throne, left the affairs of the empire to his ministers, and retired to attend to his pursuit of spiritual perfection. He obtained it, and ascended to the heavens astride a yellow dragon, for all his subjects to see.

Name _____ Date _____

Respond to Reading

Read each question. Circle the letter next to your answer choice.

1. Some historians believe Huangdi may have been a real person. Therefore, this story is best characterized as which genre?

   a. a tall tale   **c.** a legend

   b. a biography   **d.** a myth

2. Read the following excerpt from the story.

   > The Yellow Emperor loved the rare creatures that lived in the mountains and was accompanied wherever he went by a procession of animals.

   Based on the text, which word would be the best substitute for the word *procession?*

   f. parade   **h.** family

   g. tribe   **j.** multitude

3. Which detail from the story supports the idea that the Yellow Emperor cared deeply about his people?

   a. He traveled in an ivory chariot pulled by dragons and an elephant.

   b. He gave the people useful items such as wheeled vehicles and calendars.

   c. He used war drums made of the skins of monsters to defeat his enemy Chi You.

   d. He rose to the heavens on the back of a great yellow dragon.

4. What is the main idea of "The Yellow Emperor"?

   f. Legend says that the Yellow Emperor, Huangdi, ruled for 100 years until a dragon took him back to heaven where he belonged.

   g. The Yellow Emperor, Huangdi, is renowned as a military leader and respected for uniting the ancient tribes of the Yellow River plain.

   h. The world would have no music if the Yellow Emperor, Huangdi, had not invented instruments such as the drum and lyre.

   j. The Yellow Emperor, Huangdi, is regarded as the creator of Chinese civilization and the ancestor of all Chinese.

Reread the story "The Yellow Emperor" on pages 113–114.

Think about what the author chose to include in this story—and what is not included. Compare and contrast the features of a legend, myth, and tall tale. Explain why this story is best described as a legend and not another genre. What characteristics of a legend are present in this selection? In what ways is this story similar to a myth or tall tale? Organize your ideas. Use the space below for prewriting.

Write about the things that make this story a legend and not a myth or tall tale. Explain your answer with details from the story. Use your own paper or a paper provided by your teacher.

Characteristic of a Legend	Example from the Story

Be sure to—

1. identify the characteristics of a legend that are present in the story.

2. explain how the features of this story distinguish it from a myth or tall tale.

3. support your ideas with details from the story that relate to the topic.

4. proofread, revise, and edit your writing as needed to improve clarity and eliminate mistakes.

Legend • *Genre Practice*

A Difficult Choice

Read the passage below. Then answer the questions that follow.

Characters

JILLIAN, age eleven

AMANI, age eleven and JILLIAN'S best friend

MOM, JILLIAN'S mother

Scene 1

(The stage is divided. Each side is decorated to look like each girl's bedroom. Two twin beds face the audience. Jillian is sitting on one bed, reading a book. A cell phone is on her nightstand. Amani is sitting on the other bed, holding a cell phone to her ear. The curtain opens with the sound of a ringing cell phone.)

JILLIAN: *(looks at cell phone and then answers)* Hey, Amani.

AMANI: Jillian, are you sitting down? If you're not sitting down, sit down NOW!

JILLIAN: *(laughing)* Yes, I'm sitting. What is it?

AMANI: OK, so my mom's office had a drawing, and they drew her name.

JILLIAN: Cool, what did she win?

AMANI: Are you still sitting?

JILLIAN: Yes, tell me.

AMANI: Tickets to see the Stars play the Dragons in the quarterfinals on Saturday!

JILLIAN: Oh, wow, Amani, that's super exciting.

AMANI: But wait, I haven't told you the best part. My mom won four tickets, one for her, for Dad, for me, and . . . for YOU!

JILLIAN: Me? You're inviting me?

AMANI: Well, yeah, who else loves basketball as much as I do?

JILLIAN: *(stands up on bed and begins to jump up and down)* Oh boy, oh boy, oh boy! Woo hoo, we're going to see the Stars!

Scene 2

(Living room in Jillian's house. A sofa is facing the audience. Jillian's mother is wearing glasses and sitting on the sofa with a computer on her lap, typing. Jillian rushes into the room.)

JILLIAN: Mom . . . Mom . . . MOM!

MOM: *(finally stops typing and looks up from computer)* Yes, Jillian.

JILLIAN: I have the absolute best news.

MOM: Is that so? And what . . .

JILLIAN: *(interrupting)* I'm going to see the Stars play in the quarterfinals with Amani!

MOM: Really? That is good news. When is the game?

JILLIAN: This Saturday.

MOM: This Saturday? The Saturday when we have plans to go to Wonder World?

JILLIAN: Wonder World is this Saturday?

MOM: I'm afraid so, sweetie. But I tell you what, if you really want to go to the game, you can. It's your decision. *(begins to type on computer again)*

JILLIAN: *(slowly lowers herself to sit in a chair, deflated)* Wonder World or the Stars? How can I choose? It's like catching my shadow. What should I do, Mom?

MOM: *(looks up, closes computer, and removes glasses)* Listen, this isn't my decision. It's yours, and it's a tough one, but you must decide which is more important to you— the Stars or Wonder World. Why don't you tell me why you like them? That might help you decide which one is more important.

JILLIAN: *(reluctantly)* OK, well, Wonder World is fun and . . .

MOM: *(encouraging)* Try to be specific. What about Wonder World would you miss if you didn't go?

JILLIAN: They have that new ride, the Shock Wave.

MOM: Good, now what about the basketball game?

JILLIAN: Well, it's the quarterfinals. And the Stars don't always make it so far in the championship series, and . . .

MOM: And?

JILLIAN: And I guess I have my decision. Wonder World and the Shock Wave will be there for another weekend, but the quarterfinals game won't. I'm going to see the Stars!

Play • *Genre Practice*

Respond to Reading

Read each question. Circle the letter next to your answer choice.

1. How do you know this passage is a play?

    a. The events are made up.

    b. It includes a description of the setting.

    c. It has dialogue meant to be spoken aloud.

    d. A character solves a problem.

2. Read the following excerpt from the selection.

    > **JILLIAN:** (*slowly lowers herself to sit in a chair, deflated*) Wonder World or the Stars? How can I choose? It's like catching my shadow. What should I do, Mom?

    The playwright's use of figurative language emphasizes that Jillian—

    f. finds it difficult to make a decision.

    g. will do whatever her mother tells her to do.

    h. prefers the activity that takes place outside.

    j. will argue she can do both activities.

3. The stage directions in Scene 2 reveal Jillian's mother—

    a. wants Jillian to spend time with her family.

    b. is interested in helping Jillian.

    c. wishes Jillian would let her work.

    d. is concerned that Jillian will be angry with her.

4. Which sentence best summarizes Scene 1?

    f. Jillian and Amani are best friends who both like basketball.

    g. Amani is excited her mom won a contest and tells Jillian.

    h. Jillian and Amani like to talk to each other on the phone.

    j. Amani has tickets to a basketball game and invites Jillian.

Reread "A Difficult Choice" on pages 117–118.

Think about how the two scenes are different. What is the purpose of each scene? Organize your ideas. Use the chart below for prewriting.

Write an essay explaining why the playwright organizes the play in two scenes. Use specific examples from the play. Use your own sheet of paper.

Scene 1 Details	Scene 2 Details

How are the two scenes different?

Be sure to—

1. explain why the playwright divides the play into two scenes.

2. provide specific examples from the play.

3. connect ideas with linking words, such as *also, another,* and *but.*

4. use correct spelling, capitalization, punctuation, and grammar.

Play • *Genre Practice*

Sisyphus

Read the passage below. Then answer the questions that follow.

Sisyphus, the King of Corinth, was considered the cleverest ruler in ancient Greece, for he often played tricks on the gods and got away with them—that is, until the day the gods exacted their revenge.

One day Sisyphus sought solitude in the woods so he could think of a plan to bring much-needed fresh water to his kingdom. As Sisyphus wandered, he spied the mighty god Zeus flying away from the forest with a beautiful water nymph. Shortly after, Sisyphus encountered Asopus, the river god, who called to Sisyphus with great urgency, "Have you seen my daughter? She's missing!"

"Yes, I have," Sisyphus replied, "and I'll tell you where I saw her—if you will supply my kingdom with a source of fresh water."

Asopus sighed. "Sisyphus, your tricky ways will cause you trouble with the gods someday. But I must get my daughter back safely, so I'll agree to your demand. Very well, Corinth now has an eternal spring that will never run dry." Sisyphus then told Asopus his daughter was with Zeus.

When Zeus learned Sisyphus was the one who alerted Asopus, Zeus became so enraged he instructed his brother Hades to take Sisyphus to the Underworld immediately. But Sisyphus predicted Zeus's plan, and formed his own cunning one. Sisyphus told his wife that soon he would appear to be dead, but that she should not worry. She should not place a gold coin under his tongue, as was the tradition in Greece.

As expected, Sisyphus died, but when he entered the Underworld, he did not have payment to enter as a king. Hades was disturbed. "Why did your wife not provide you with a gold coin so that you could enter the Underworld as royalty? I've never seen such behavior before."

Seemingly humiliated, Sisyphus replied, "My wife chose not to pay for my passage."

Hades bellowed, "Then you will return to Earth, retrieve the coin from her, and come back to the Underworld as the king you are. Now go!" Sisyphus thanked Hades and without hesitation, exited the Underworld.

Upon his return to Earth, Sisyphus reunited with his wife, who was overjoyed to see him, and relayed the story of how he had tricked Hades into allowing him to return to her. Sisyphus had no intention of going back to the Underworld; he lived many more years until finally dying of old age.

But this is not the end of Sisyphus's story. When Sisyphus entered the Underworld a second time, Hades was waiting for him. Sternly, Hades said, "Sisyphus, for all your offenses against the gods, especially those against me and my brother Zeus, you will be punished. Your punishment is to roll this boulder to the top of the mountain."

Sisyphus had no more tricks. He accepted his punishment and began to roll the massive boulder up the steep hill. The task was exhausting, but Sisyphus persevered and was almost to top when the boulder rolled back down. Sisyphus attempted to push the rock up the mountain again, but once more it rolled back down.

You see, Sisyphus's punishment was not to roll the boulder up the mountain only once but to roll the boulder up the mountain over and over for all eternity. As clever as Sisyphus was, he could never really outsmart the gods.

Myth • *Genre Practice*

Respond to Reading

Read each question. Circle the letter next to your answer choice.

1. What makes this selection a myth?

    a. A human interacts with gods.

    b. One character tricks other characters.

    c. Events are repeated.

    d. Real places are named.

2. Read the following excerpt.

    > You see, Sisyphus's punishment was not to roll the boulder up the mountain only once but to roll the boulder up the mountain over and over, for all eternity.

    Which word or words from the excerpt help you understand the meaning of *eternity*?

    f. punishment

    g. to roll the boulder up

    h. once

    j. over and over

3. Sisyphus tells his wife not to put a gold coin under his tongue when he dies because—

    a. she does not have a gold coin to spare.

    b. he believes the tradition is foolish and should be discontinued.

    c. he knows Hades will not allow him in the Underworld without one.

    d. it will get lost in the Underworld.

4. What lesson does Sisyphus learn?

    f. Two people can benefit from a compromise.

    g. Be careful how you treat others as they might treat you the same way.

    h. Make sure to always carry money.

    j. Anger can lead to forgiveness when people admit their mistakes.

Reread "Sisyphus" on pages 121–122.

Think about Sisyphus's actions, thoughts, and words. What makes Sisyphus clever? Organize your ideas. Use the space below for prewriting.

Write an essay explaining how the author supports the idea that Sisyphus is the "cleverest ruler in ancient Greece." Use specific evidence from the selection. Use your own sheet of paper.

_____

_____

_____

_____

_____

_____

_____

_____

_____

_____

_____

Be sure to—

1. explain how the author supports the idea that Sisyphus is clever.

2. provide evidence from the selection.

3. use linking words, such as *also, another,* and *but.*

4. use correct spelling, capitalization, punctuation, and grammar.

Myth • *Genre Practice*

Dolphin Speak

Read both selections. Then answer the questions that follow.

Most people know dolphins are among the most intelligent mammals on Earth. But did you know that some scientists believe dolphins can "talk" to one another in their own special language? For decades, researchers have been trying to crack the secret code of "dolphin speak."

From the time they're born, dolphins make a wide variety of noises. Scientists have names for each one: chuff, pop, squeak, click, whistle, and squawk. Each sound may have a different meaning. Dolphins also appear to use a form of body language to communicate: caressing or biting one another's fins, bobbing their heads, and blowing bubbles. Researchers believe dolphins use these vocalizations and physical and visual signals to communicate all sorts of things, from their feelings (anger, frustration, or affection) to their age and gender.

Each dolphin may also have a unique "signature whistle" it uses to identify itself, functioning almost like a personal name.

Kathleen Dudzinski of the Dolphin Communication Project says one reason decoding "dolphin speak" is difficult is because the same sounds and gestures seem to have different meanings depending on what the dolphins are doing. A squeak or whistle during a fight might mean something very different than the same sound during a play session. But Dudzinski points out that the same is true for people: When you say, "This ice cream is cool," for example, are you saying it's slightly cold or that it's totally awesome?

Scientists do not believe dolphin language is akin to human language. Dolphins are not likely chatting about the weather or sports teams as they swim. But even if they don't have a human language, dolphins do have a sophisticated way of communicating—and researchers are learning more and more about it every day.

Swimming with Dolphins

Not too many people get to play with dolphins. But this summer my family visited an aquarium in Florida that has a special Dolphin Encounter program. I've always loved dolphins, and when I heard about the program, I knew we'd have to make it part of our vacation.

When we arrived at the aquarium, we went into a special room to see a video about how to interact with the dolphins. The video said we should never touch their eyes or their blowholes. A blowhole is the dolphin's nostril on the top of its head, which it uses to breathe air just like we do. Dolphins aren't fish, you know. They're mammals like us.

When the video ended, a marine biologist gave everyone life jackets, wetsuits, and flippers. Then she led us out into a large pool to meet the dolphins. The water was about waist-deep, and I have to admit it smelled really bad—salty and fishy. But that's the kind of water dolphins like.

All of a sudden, I saw a dolphin swimming right toward me—gray and white with the smoothest-looking skin I've ever seen. I forgot all about how smelly the water was. I was a little scared to see such a big creature coming right at me, but he was really friendly. The biologist said his name was Freddy. She gave Freddy a command, and he whistled and held his head up out of the water right in front of me. "Go ahead and give him a kiss if you want," she said. So I leaned down and kissed him, right on his bottle nose!

We played with Freddy for about thirty minutes. I fed him a fish, tossed him some toys (which he brought back to me), and we even sang a song together. Before we left, the biologist taught me the command for Freddy to "shake hands," and he swam right up to me and held out his fin. It was so much fun! I hope you have the chance to swim with the dolphins one day.

Comparing Genres • *Genre Practice*

Respond to Reading

Read each question. Circle the letter next to your answer choice.

1. The selection "Dolphin Speak" is best characterized as—
   a. informational writing, because it contains facts.
   b. argumentative writing, because includes an emotional appeal to the reader.
   c. descriptive writing, because the writer uses sensory details to paint a picture for the reader.
   d. persuasive writing, because it expresses the writer's opinion about a topic.

2. What is the main idea of the selection "Dolphin Speak"?
   f. Dolphin language is very much like human language.
   g. Dolphins have a language for communicating with each other.
   h. Researchers understand the meaning of all the sounds dolphins make.
   j. Humans and dolphins can "speak" to each other.

3. What kind of writing is "Swimming with Dolphins"?
   a. It is an autobiography, because it is the story of a real person's life written by that person.
   b. It is persuasive writing, because it is meant to make readers think in a certain way.
   c. It is an adventure tale, because it is an exciting story about realistic characters and places.
   d. It is narrative nonfiction, because it is a story about a real event that happened to the writer.

4. In the story "Swimming with Dolphins," what is the LAST thing the writer did with Freddy?
   f. shook his fin
   g. kissed his nose
   h. fed him a fish
   j. sang a song with him

5. What is one way the two selections are similar?

  a. They both blend elements of fiction and nonfiction.

  b. They both are about real people and real animals.

  c. They both express an opinion intended to persuade the reader.

  d. They both use imagination to tell a story.

6. What is one difference between the two selections?

  f. Only one includes an emotional appeal.

  g. Only one is nonfiction.

  h. Only one is organized in chronological order.

  j. Only one provides factual information.

7. Which idea is found in both selections?

  a. Dolphins breathe air just like people.

  b. Dolphins are intelligent, fascinating creatures.

  c. Dolphins eat fish like herring, cod, or mackerel.

  d. Dolphins can be trained to do tricks.

8. Which idea is found in only one of the selections?

  f. Like people, dolphins are a kind of mammal.

  g. Researchers believe dolphin language is as complex as human language.

  h. Dolphins breathe through a special opening in their head called a blowhole.

  j. Some scientists think dolphin whistles act as a dolphin's "name."

Comparing Genres • *Genre Practice*

Name _____ **Date** _____

Comparing Genres

Reread the selections "Dolphin Speak" and "Swimming with Dolphins" on pages 125–126.

Think about each author's purpose. How successfully does each author achieve that purpose? What does each author want you to think about dolphins? Is one selection more entertaining or informative than the other? Organize your ideas. Use the space below for prewriting.

Write about which of the selections you liked the best and why. Give evidence from the selections to support your ideas. Use your own paper or a paper provided by your teacher.

	"Dolphin Speak"	**"Swimming with Dolphins"**
Why did the author write this selection?		
What did you learn about dolphins from this selection?		
How entertaining or informative was this selection? Why do you think this?		

Be sure to—

1. describe each author's purpose and how successfully that purpose was achieved.

2. tell what you learned about dolphins from each selection.

3. state an opinion about which selection you liked the best.

4. support your opinion with details from the selections that relate to the topic.

5. proofread, revise, and edit your writing as needed to improve clarity and eliminate mistakes.

Revising

Use this checklist to revise your opinion writing.

- Does your writing have a clear purpose?
- Does your writing state an opinion?
- Does your writing have reasons that support your opinion?
- Does your writing include interesting details or descriptions?
- Did you include an ending that sums up your opinion?

Editing/Proofreading

Use this checklist to correct mistakes in your opinion writing.

- Did you use proofreading symbols when editing?
- Does your writing include transition words?
- Did you check for subject/verb agreement?
- Did you check your writing for spelling mistakes?

Publishing

Use this checklist to prepare your opinion writing for publishing.

- Write or type a neat copy of your writing.
- Add a photograph or a drawing if it enhances your writing.

Comparing Genres • *Genre Practice*

Conundrum Tower

**Read the passage below. Then answer the questions
that follow.**

"We should turn back," Adlet exclaimed. "There's no tower out here." She glared at Tiak, slowing her pace to demonstrate her displeasure. "We've been in these woods for hours!"

Tiak shook his head and grunted, striding ahead resolutely. "If Conundrum Tower isn't real, why do the elders insist we never seek it out? There MUST be something out here . . ."

Adlet spat scornfully. "They tell the young ones that flower elves leave sweets under their pillow on Planting Day. Do you still believe THAT?"

Before Tiak could reply, Iclyn tugged at the hem of Adlet's tunic. "Just a little farther?" she pleaded.

Adlet's face softened as she gazed at her younger sister. "Your first adventure, yeah?" she smiled. "I'd forgotten you've never before ventured into Jade Forest." She stopped to kneel beside Iclyn, caressing her long, platinum hair.

"Not my first!" Iclyn replied. "Remember last winter when Glistening Pond was frozen over—"

"—and Tiak rescued you when it gave way beneath you," Adlet finished quietly, pulling Iclyn close. "All right, brave girl. We'll keep going for now, but when the sun reaches Iron Bluff we'll need to—"

"Hey! Look what I've found!"

While the girls were talking, Tiak had hiked into a clearing . . . and there it was: Conundrum Tower. He paused to smile at Adlet triumphantly as she and Iclyn joined him. Adlet barely glanced his way as she pushed past him, eyes wide, to approach the high stone structure. She picked her way through the bricks that littered the twisting path to the tower, Tiak and Iclyn trailing close behind.

A battered oaken door confronted the adventurers at the tower's base, a large question mark carved into its face. As Tiak traced the question mark with his fingertips, the door creaked open. Adlet and Tiak peered into the darkness skeptically, while Iclyn gripped her sister's hand. Finally, Adlet spoke, "Well, we've come this far."

Grinning, Tiak stepped across the threshold. Adlet quickly followed, pulling Iclyn in with her. Instantly, the door slammed shut. Torches along the walls flared into life, dimly illuminating the room to reveal broken arrows, rusty swords, and empty flasks, forgotten and defaced by time itself. At the far end of the room, a moss-covered statue stood guard.

Before the trio could react, the statue blinked and looked quizzically at them. Then it began to murmur, "Only those who can unwind my riddle may leave Conundrum Tower:

> *The wave, over the wave, a weird thing I saw,*
> *A wonder on the wave—water became bone.*"

And with that, the statue again lapsed into stony silence.

"What!?" Tiak hissed in a panic. "Those words have no meaning!"

"How can we reply to a question that has no answer?" Adlet shouted to the statue before shaking her fist at Tiak. "I told you we should have turned back!"

"Let us out!" yelled Tiak, pounding on the closed door.

But as Tiak and Adlet raged behind her, Iclyn looked thoughtful. "Water . . . hard like bone . . . ," she whispered to herself. "Like . . . Glistening Pond!"

She took a step toward the statue. "Is it . . . ice?"

The figure smiled and nodded . . . and in an instant the tower door flew open. Heads spinning, the adventurers scrambled out into the late afternoon sun, the door slamming behind them.

"Iclyn!" Tiak cried, hoisting the blushing girl onto his shoulders. "You're our hero!"

"I . . . I wonder what the flower elves will leave us on Planting Day," Adlet muttered as the three began their journey back home.

Fantasy • *Genre Practice*

Respond to Reading

Read each question. Circle the letter next to your answer choice.

1. "Conundrum Tower" is best characterized as a(n)—
   a. tall tale, because it uses humorous exaggeration to tell a story.
   b. adventure tale, because it includes action and suspense.
   c. fable, because the characters learn something at the end.
   d. fantasy, because things happen that could not happen in the real world.

2. Read the following sentence from the story.

   > "I . . . I wonder what the flower elves will leave us on Planting Day," Adlet muttered as the three began their journey back home.

   This sentence supports the idea that Adlet—
   f. wants a treat after her experience in Conundrum Tower.
   g. is angry with Tiak for believing the Planting Day story.
   h. has gained newfound respect for the teachings of the elders.
   j. is grateful to her younger sister for solving the riddle.

3. Which detail from the story best explains why Iclyn is able to solve the riddle?
   a. Adlet wants to give up searching for Conundrum Tower, but Iclyn wants to keep going.
   b. Iclyn had fallen through the frozen pond the previous winter.
   c. Adlet has to pull the reluctant Iclyn into Conundrum Tower.
   d. Iclyn has never before ventured into Jade Forest.

4. The title of the story helps the reader understand that—
   f. a riddle or puzzle will be a major part of the action.
   g. the three adventurers will barely escape an awful fate.
   h. the youngest of the characters will be the hero.
   j. the story will have a happy ending.

Reread the story "Conundrum Tower" on pages 131–132.

Think about the words and actions of each character. What do their words and actions tell you about their personalities? What does the author want you to think about them? Do any characters change from the beginning to the end of the story? How have they changed by the end of the story? Organize your ideas. Use the space below for prewriting.

Write about the personalities of the three main characters in this story. Explain your answer with details from the story. Use your own paper or a paper provided by your teacher.

	Adlet	**Tiak**	**Iclyn**
Character's words			
Character's actions			
Based on the character's words and actions, how would you describe the character's personality?			
Evidence the character changes by the end of the story			

Be sure to—

1. describe each character's personality, using evidence from the story.

2. explain how characters changed by the end of the story.

3. support your ideas with details from the story that relate to the topic.

4. proofread, revise, and edit your writing as needed to improve clarity and eliminate mistakes.

Fantasy • *Genre Practice*

Should Young People Work?

**Read the selection below. Then answer the questions
that follow.**

Just like grownups, young people want things. Their favorite band produces a new
album, and they want to download the songs. Their sneakers are worn, and they
want a new pair. A new electronic gadget appears on the market, and they want the
updated technology. The problem with all these wants is that they cost money. What's
a kid to do? One solution is for young people to have paying jobs.

By age twelve, many young people will earn money by way of informal jobs, such
as babysitting, pet walking, or lawn mowing. As kids grow older, they may transition
to more formal jobs, like working as an amusement park attendant, a camp counselor,
a waiter, or a cashier in a grocery store. Sometimes, teens work all year but only part-
time. Other times, teens work full-time but only during the summer. By law, teens of a
certain age are allowed to work, but should they?

While jobs provide young people with money, teen employment also has drawbacks.
For those teens who work during the school year, having a job after school means
less time for homework, which could result in poorer grades. Another drawback to
working is that having a job may cause extra stress, especially when trying to balance
work, school, extracurricular activities, and free time. Are lower grades in school and
increased stress worth having money to spend? Some would say no.

Others, though, would say that teens benefit from employment as long as they
work part-time. One benefit, in fact, is higher, not lower, grades. While studies have
shown that teens who worked more than twenty hours each week did have lower
grades, the grades of teens who worked less than twenty hours each week did not
suffer. In fact, those teens earned higher grades than teens who worked more hours
and teens who did not work at all. That's because moderately employed teens
who still had time for homework, gained confidence and practiced responsibility
while working. In turn, they transferred these skills to their schoolwork and achieved
better grades.

Another benefit of working part-time is more obvious—money. Teens who have part-time jobs are able to contribute to the purchase of things they want and need. They do not have to ask their parents for money as often. Earning money also teaches young people how to manage money. For example, because one paycheck will not cover the total cost of a new cell phone, a teen will need to save money each pay period until they've saved enough to purchase the phone. Moreover, having teens spend their own money teaches them just how much things cost. Before having a job, one teen might not have thought twice about spending $25 on a shirt. After having a job, though, that teen understands the cost of the shirt equals more than two hours of work.

A final benefit for young people working part-time is that a job provides a constructive way for teens to fill their free time. Some teens find themselves with nothing to do after school. A part-time job, though, gives teens an activity, an activity that not only boosts their confidence and enables them to practice real-world skills, but also allows them to earn money.

For those young people who want things and need money to buy them, having a part-time job is a good solution. While the money teens earn is important, the other benefits they gain are valuable too.

Argumentative Text • *Genre Practice*

Respond to Reading

Read each question. Circle the letter next to your answer choice.

1. The main purpose of this selection is to—

   a. describe the different jobs available to young people.

   b. persuade others that working can benefit young people.

   c. show others how young people are responsible.

   d. explain the reasons why young people want to work.

2. Read the following excerpt.

   > That's because moderately employed teens who still had time for homework, gained confidence and practiced responsibility while working.

   What does the word *moderately* mean?

   f. noticeably   h. overly

   g. slightly   j. extremely

3. The author includes the description of a teen buying a cell phone in the fifth paragraph most likely to—

   a. explain one way a teen would spend money earned from a job.

   b. show a teen who wants the latest technology.

   c. provide an example of a teen learning how to manage money.

   d. describe a problem a teen faces when working.

4. Which sentence from the selection best expresses the author's main idea?

   f. While jobs provide young people with money, teen employment also has drawbacks.

   g. One benefit, in fact, is higher, not lower, grades.

   h. Earning money also teaches teens how to manage money.

   j. For those young people who want things and need money to buy them, having a part-time job is a good solution.

Reread the fourth, fifth, and sixth paragraphs of "Should Young People Work?" on pages 135–136.

Think about the reasons and evidence the author provides as arguments for teens to have part-time jobs. Use the graphic organizer below for prewriting.

Write an explanation of how the author supports his or her claim. Which reasons and evidence does the author provide? Are they convincing? Use specific examples from the selection. Use your own sheet of paper.

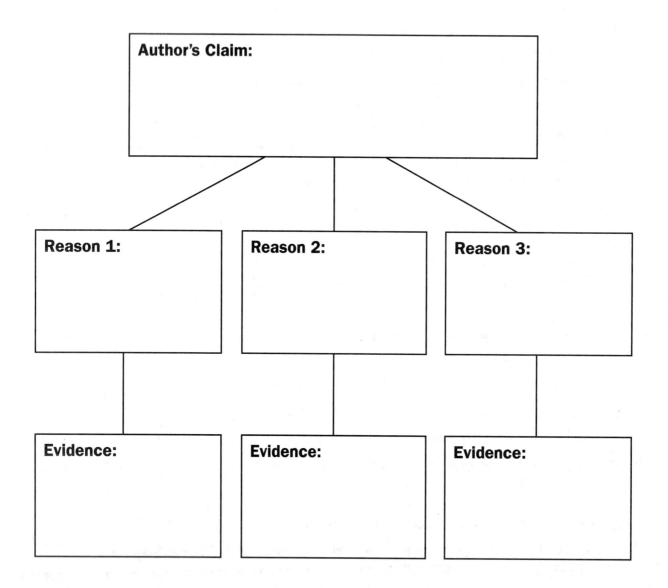

Be sure to—

1. explain how the author supports his or her claim.

2. include evidence from the selection.

3. connect ideas using linking words, such as *also, another,* and *but.*

4. use correct spelling, capitalization, punctuation, and grammar.

Argumentative Text • *Genre Practice*

The Jackalope

Read the selection below. Then answer the questions that follow.

Tales of a beast that is as sly as a fox and as fierce as a lion have circulated throughout the Old West. American cowboys were the first to encounter this creature, but seeing one now would be like spotting a mermaid or Bigfoot. What is this mysterious animal? Why, it's a jackalope, of course.

The jackalope is a cross between a jackrabbit and an antelope, or a rabbit with antlers. Jackalopes, though, are not born with antlers. The antlers appear shortly after a young jackalope leaves its mother. Jackalope mothers' milk is highly valued due its powerful healing capabilities. For example, one bald man grew a full head of hair after drinking one glass of jackalope milk.

However, extracting milk from a jackalope is not advised, as they become quite aggressive when cornered. Jackalopes are known as "warrior rabbits" and will use their antlers for defense. People who enjoy danger and decide they'd like to attempt milking a jackalope should wait until the jackalope is sleeping belly up. Then, they can try to sneak up on it. These daring people should also wear protective gear on their calves in case the jackalope wakes up and begins to attack. Stovepipes serve as good protection for the legs, but they can make a lot of noise when walking. Therefore, it's important to practice walking in them before even attempting to approach a sleeping jackalope. Not even a snake is meaner than an agitated jackalope.

For the most part, though, jackalopes are shy animals and will flee rather than fight. Catching jackalopes is a difficult task because not only are they fast—so fast the human eye cannot keep track of them—but they are also clever. Jackalopes combine their speed and wit with their ability to mimic human voices to avoid capture. When chased, jackalopes often shout out phrases such as "There he goes over there," "Look to your right," and "Now on your left" in order to baffle their pursuers.

One method for catching a jackalope has been proven successful, and that is to wait for a full moon. When jackalopes see a full moon rising, they believe it is the setting sun. This confuses the jackalopes; they think the evening is rewinding. As such, the jackalopes begin to "rewind" themselves by walking backward and in circles. With their speed and range tremendously reduced, the jackalopes become easier to snatch. However, they do not make good pets.

While jackalopes once freely roamed the entire American West, they are now, unfortunately, thought to be extinct. Even so, recent jackalope sightings have been reported in Oregon, Nebraska, and Wyoming, which leads researchers to believe that pockets of jackalope communities still survive.

Douglas, Wyoming, is one such town where jackalopes likely reside. In fact, Douglas claims that the very first jackalope sighting took place there in 1829. For this reason, Douglas is often called the Jackalope Capital of America. A large concrete statue of a jackalope stands in the center of town, and Douglas holds a jackalope festival each June. Locals and tourists alike attend the festival, eager to spot just one of these quick and crafty critters, as though that's a difficult thing to do.

Name _____ Date _____

Respond to Reading

Read each question. Circle the letter next to your answer choice.

1. What makes this selection a tall tale?

    a. real places

    b. a mystery characters must solve

    c. an animal as a main character

    d. humorous exaggerations

2. Read the following excerpt.

    > American cowboys were the first to encounter this creature, but seeing one now would be like spotting a mermaid or Bigfoot. What is this mysterious animal? Why, it's a jackalope, of course.

    The author uses figurative language to tell readers—

    f. that seeing a jackalope would be rare.

    g. why cowboys were the first to see a jackalope.

    h. the different sizes of jackalopes.

    j. how jackalopes are identified.

3. Why must people practice walking with stovepipes around their legs before approaching a jackalope?

    a. So they can discover the correct size of stovepipes for their legs.

    b. So they don't make too much noise and wake up a jackalope.

    c. So they don't look foolish and start laughing.

    d. So they can run when a jackalope attacks.

4. Which of these statements is an important idea explored in this selection?

    f. Jackalopes can be caught only at night under a full moon.

    g. Jackalopes are peculiar animals with varying actions and powers.

    h. Jackalopes were first discovered in Douglas, Wyoming.

    j. Jackalope milk can be used to treat many different conditions.

Reread the first paragraph on page 140.

Think about the words the author uses to set up opposing ideas. What idea is being contradicted in this paragraph? How does a contradiction help the author develop a tall tale? Organize your ideas. Use the chart below for prewriting.

Write an explanation of how the author's use of contradiction contributes to the tall tale. Use specific evidence from the selection. Use your own sheet of paper.

Author first says . . .	Then the author says . . .

The contradiction helps develop the tall tale because . . .

Be sure to—

1. explain how the author's use of contradiction contributes to the tall tale.

2. support your ideas with evidence from the selection.

3. use linking words, such as *also, another,* and *but.*

4. use correct spelling, capitalization, punctuation, and grammar.

Tall Tale • *Genre Practice*

The Trees and the Axe

Read the passage below. Then answer the questions that follow.

A man wandered into a dense forest one afternoon, looking this way and that as though he was searching for something. Few ever ventured so deeply into the woods, and the Trees, being naturally curious, called out to him:

"Excuse us, stranger! It looks as though you want something. Can we help in any way?"

"Oh, kind Trees," the man replied. "I just knew you would help me. You see, all I want is a piece of hard, solid wood to make a handle for my axe." He held up the axe head pitifully. "You see that it's no good without a handle."

The good-natured Trees chuckled. "Why, what a modest request!" the oldest Trees whispered among themselves. "If that is all he requires we can surely provide it, and then he will be content to go on his way and leave the rest of us be." Without hesitation they voted to sacrifice a young ash sapling and offered it to the man. The little sapling objected meekly, but the older trees ignored its appeals.

"Thank you!" the man cried gratefully, wasting no time fashioning the sapling into a handle and fitting it into the axe head. The trees watched him work, eager for him to finish. All this commotion was disturbing their privacy!

But no sooner had the man fixed the handle into the axe head than he began to use it, and he set to work cutting down tree after tree. Maples, sycamores, cedars—the woodsman's axe spared none of them. He worked so quickly that his strokes felled several giants before the Trees quite realized how the man was using their gift.

Only then did the Trees understand how foolish they had been. "Alas!" cried an ancient oak, bemoaning to a neighboring beech the destruction of his companions, "If only we had not given up the ash sapling, we might ourselves have stood for ages and ages more."

Respond to Reading

Read each question. Circle the letter next to your answer choice.

1. "The Trees and the Axe" is best characterized as a—

   a. myth, because it explains why people behave in certain ways.

   b. legend, because it is based on a real person who lived long ago.

   c. fairy tale, because it involves creatures with magical powers.

   d. fable, because it is very short and teaches a lesson.

2. Read the following excerpt.

   > A man wandered into a dense forest one afternoon, looking this way and that as though he was searching for something.

   Which word could replace *dense* in this sentence?

   f. thick
   h. quiet

   g. hot
   j. lonely

3. What do the trees hope to accomplish by giving the man the young ash sapling?

   a. They intend to rid themselves of the grumpy ash sapling.

   b. They hope the man will be satisfied and leave the rest of them alone.

   c. They want the man to think they are generous and kind.

   d. They wish to give the man a gift for visiting them.

4. What would be the best moral for this story?

   f. Many pretend to hate what is beyond their reach.

   g. Those who sacrifice the rights of others may lose their own rights.

   h. Never trust a friend who leaves you when trouble approaches.

   j. There is always someone worse off than you.

Reread the story "The Trees and the Axe" on pages 143–144.

Think about the motivations and actions of the Trees. How do their actions affect them in the end? What does the author want you to think about the Trees? How could the author have written the story to give the Trees a better ending? Organize your ideas. Use the space below for prewriting.

Write about how the behavior of the Trees impacts the moral of the story. If the author wanted the moral of the story to be "United we stand, divided we fall," how might the Trees have behaved differently? Explain your answer with details from the story. Use your own paper or a paper provided by your teacher.

What the Trees Do	How the Trees' Actions Affect Them

Be sure to—

1. describe how the actions of the Trees affects them.

2. explain the relationship between the actions of the Trees and the moral of the story.

3. tell what the Trees could have done differently to teach a lesson on unity.

4. support your ideas with details from the story that relate to the topic.

5. proofread, revise, and edit your writing as needed to improve clarity and eliminate mistakes.

Fable • *Genre Practice*

Basket Case

Read the passage below. Then answer the questions that follow.

Characters

RAMON, an elementary school student
KATIE, a classmate
EMILY, another classmate
JAMAL, an older elementary school student

(The school playground at recess. Ramon is shooting baskets by himself when his classmate, Katie, approaches, grabs a rebound, and begins dribbling the ball.)

RAMON: *(angrily)* Hey, give me the ball!

KATIE: *(teasingly)* Why should I? (*smiles, continues dribbling*)

RAMON: *(approaches Katie)* Because I said so. Come on, I had it first.

KATIE: *(stops dribbling, looks a bit confused)* Why can't I play with you? We shot baskets together yesterday.

RAMON: *(getting up in Katie's face)* 'Cause I don't want you to, that's why.

KATIE: *(raising her voice)* You don't own the ball, it belongs to the school!

RAMON: *(grabbing the ball)* I said give me the ball! (*Both begin to shout as they struggle for the ball; a crowd of kids, including Jamal and Emily, runs over to watch.*)

EMILY: Hey, you guys! (*She and Jamal step between Ramon and Katie, who separate with Ramon now in possession of the ball. Katie stands nearby with her arms crossed.*)

JAMAL: What's going on? This isn't like you, Ramon. You two seemed like best friends yesterday.

RAMON: So what? Just leave us alone!

EMILY: I'm sure we can figure out a way to solve this problem. Should we try?

(together) **KATIE:** Yes! **RAMON:** No!

JAMAL: *(looking toward the playground monitor, and then back at Ramon)* What do you think will happen if we don't solve the problem?

RAMON: *(sheepishly)* I . . . I guess I'd get in trouble . . . and maybe—

EMILY: *(interrupting)* Come on. Let's move away from the others and talk.

(The four walk to a quiet spot on the playground as the crowd of kids disperses.)

JAMAL: OK. Let's all take a deep breath. *(They all breathe deeply.)* Katie, what exactly is the problem?

KATIE: Well, I wanted to shoot baskets with Ramon, but he wouldn't let me. So I—

RAMON: *(interrupting)* It wasn't like that! First—

EMILY: Ramon, let her finish! Then you can tell your side of the story. *(turns to Katie)* Go on, Katie.

KATIE: Well, I just wanted to shoot some baskets. We played together yesterday. I don't understand why he's being so mean.

JAMAL: Talk about how *you* feel, Katie . . . it sounds like you're confused. Is that right?

KATIE: *(quietly)* Yeah.

JAMAL: OK. So Ramon, why don't you tell what the problem is and how *you* feel about it?

RAMON: I was just minding my own business shooting hoops when all of a sudden she *(glancing sharply at Katie)* came over and took the ball without even asking.

EMILY: And how do you feel about that?

RAMON: I feel like she should just leave me alone!

EMILY: But how do you *feel*?

RAMON: Well . . . I'm . . . I'm *angry!* *(He bounces the ball hard.)*

(No one speaks for a moment, and then Katie looks at Ramon.)

KATIE: *(tentatively)* Are . . . are you really that angry with me just because I wanted to play ball with you?

RAMON: *(loudly)* I just wanted to be alone! *(He looks down for a moment, and then back up at Katie.)* I had a fight with my brother before school. Maybe I was still mad about that. I . . . I just wanted to be by myself.

JAMAL: *(putting his hand on Ramon's shoulder)* So . . . you were mostly upset about your brother?

RAMON: And I guess I took it out on Katie. *(looks at her)* Hey, I'm . . . I'm sorry.

KATIE: *(quietly)* I'm sorry you were upset . . . I . . . wish you had just told me. Still friends?

RAMON: *(tossing ball to Katie)* Yeah. Still friends.

(The four walk back to the basketball hoop.)

Play • *Genre Practice*

Name _____ Date _____

Respond to Reading

Read each question. Circle the letter next to your answer choice.

1. "Basket Case" is best characterized as a play because it—

   a. has more than one character.

   b. includes dialogue and stage directions.

   c. teaches the audience a lesson or moral.

   d. is based on events that could really happen.

2. Read the following excerpt.

   > **RAMON:** (*angrily*) Hey, give me the ball!
   >
   > **KATIE:** (*teasingly*) Why should I? (*smiles, continues dribbling*)
   >
   > **RAMON:** (*approaches Katie*) Because I said so. Come on, I had it first.
   >
   > **KATIE:** (*stops dribbling, looks a bit confused*) Why can't I play with you? We shot baskets together yesterday.

   What can you infer from this conversation?

   f. Katie expects Ramon to play with her.

   g. Ramon does not like Katie.

   h. Katie tries to make Ramon angry.

   j. Ramon is a good basketball player.

3. When Katie and Ramon begin arguing, why do Jamal and Emily run over to them?

   a. They want to watch the fight between Katie and Ramon.

   b. They want to get Katie and Ramon in trouble with the playground monitor.

   c. They want to join Katie and Ramon in the basketball game.

   d. They want to help Katie and Ramon work out their differences.

4. Which statement is the best summary for "Basket Case"?

   f. Friends work together to resolve a conflict on the playground.

   g. A boy has a bad morning and takes it out on a classmate at school.

   h. A girl's feelings are hurt when a friend refuses to play with her.

   j. A fight between classmates breaks out on the playground at recess.

Genre Practice • Play

Reread the play "Basket Case" on pages 147–148.

Think about the kinds of things that can happen on a school playground. Is a playground usually crowded or mostly empty? How might the number of kids on the playground have impacted the characters' behavior? How does the setting determine how the plot is resolved? Would the story be better told in another setting? Why or why not? Organize your ideas. Use the space below for prewriting.

Write about the setting and its impact on the action of the play. Was a school playground a good choice for a story about conflict? Why or why not? How does the setting affect the way the characters behave? Might they act differently in another setting? Use your own sheet of paper to explain your answer.

Things That Happen on a School Playground	How Might This Cause Conflict?	How Might This Resolve Conflict?

Be sure to—

1. describe the setting and how it affects the characters and the plot.

2. explain why the playwright chooses this setting for the play.

3. state your opinion about the effectiveness of the play's setting.

4. support your opinion with details from the play that relate to the topic.

5. proofread, revise, and edit your writing as needed to improve clarity and eliminate mistakes.

Graphic Organizer Resources

Cause and Effect

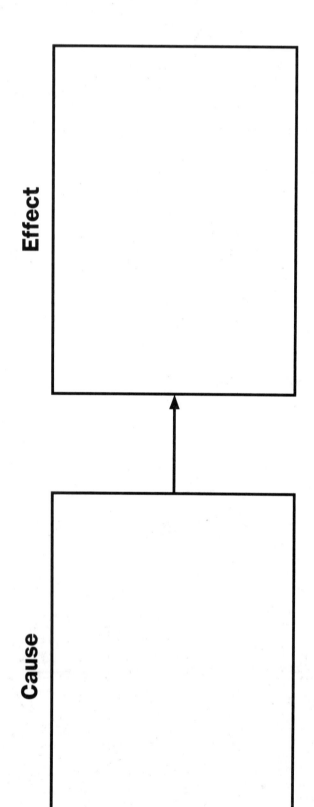

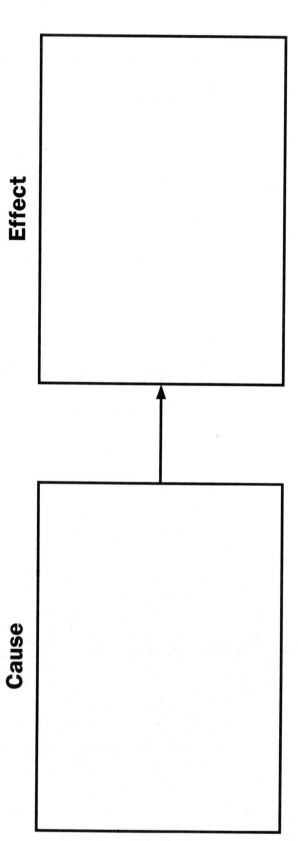

Name _____ Date _____

Compare and Contrast

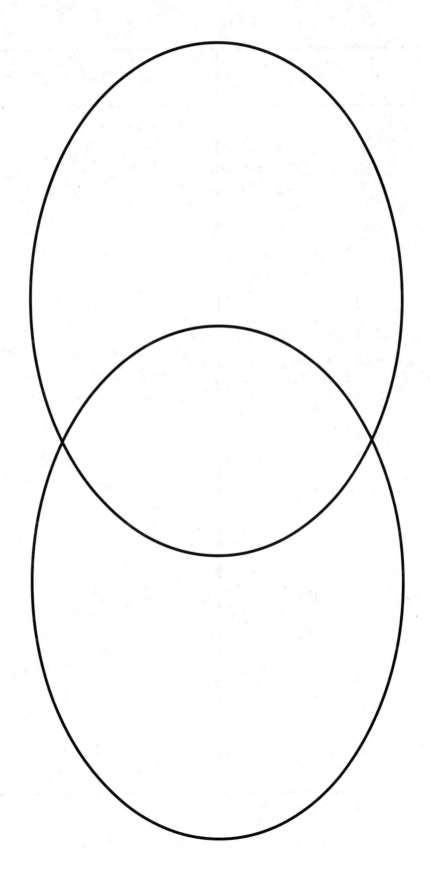

Fact and Opinion

Main Idea and Details

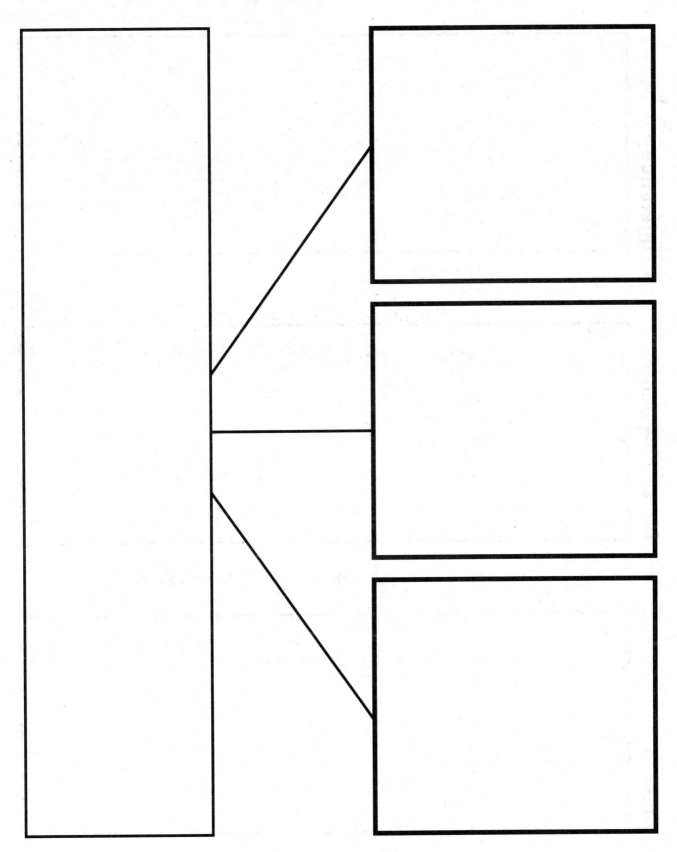

Making Inferences

Inference

=

Prior Knowledge

+

Clue

Sequence

First

Next

Last

Word Map

Plot

Solution:

Climax:

Problem:

Name _____ **Date** _____

Four-Column Chart

Idea Web

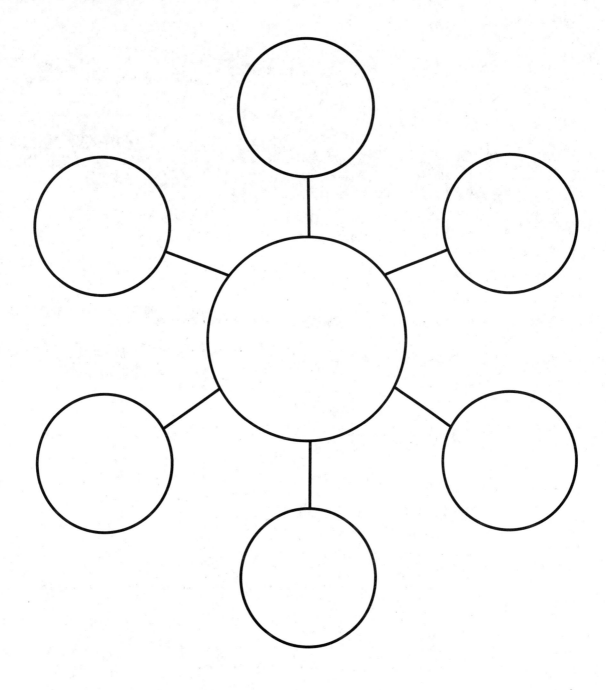